The Myths of
Standardized Tests

To our families: the Harris clan, Steven, Vicky, Janine, and Katie; the Smiths, Louise, Amanda, and Margaret whose combined experiences and input helped make this book possible. And to the memory of Gerald Bracey who spent decades educating leaders and policy makers about the myths of standardized testing.

The Myths of Standardized Tests

Why They Don't Tell You What You Think They Do

Phillip Harris, Bruce M. Smith, and Joan Harris

ROWMAN & LITTLEFIELD
Lanham • Boulder • New York • London

Published by Rowman & Littlefield Publishers, Inc.
A wholly owned subsidiary of The Rowman & Littlefield Publishing Group, Inc.
4501 Forbes Boulevard, Suite 200, Lanham, Maryland 20706
http://www.rowmanlittlefield.com

Estover Road, Plymouth PL6 7PY, United Kingdom

British Library Cataloguing in Publication Information Available

Library of Congress Cataloging-in-Publication Data

The hardback edition of this book was previously cataloged by the Library of Congress as follows:

Harris, Phillip, 1939-
  The myths of standardized tests : why they don't tell you what you think they do / Phillip Harris, Bruce M. Smith, and Joan Harris.
    p. cm.
  ISBN 978-1-4422-0809-4 (cloth : alk. paper) — ISBN 978-1-4422-0811-7 (electronic) — ISBN 978-0-8108-9614-7 (paper : alk. paper)
    1. Universities and colleges—United States—Admission. 2. Education, Higher—Standards—United States. 3. College applications—United States. I. Smith, Bruce M., 1949- II. Harris, Joan, 1938- III. Title.
  LB2351.2.H356 2011
  371.26'4—dc22

                                                                                    2010025598

∞™ The paper used in this publication meets the minimum requirements of American National Standard for Information Sciences—Permanence of Paper for Printed Library Materials, ANSI/NISO Z39.48-1992.

Printed in the United States of America

Contents

A Medley of Views

Introduction: This Is *Not* a Test

[Testing] is the mechanism we have. We may not like it.

—Tony Bennett, Indiana State Superintendent of Public Instruction, 2008

This is an actual emergency. Our schools are under attack, and with them, the future of our young people. What's more, this assault isn't being perpetrated by some foreign power bent on our destruction. No Red Hand, no Shining Path, no al-Qaida. This assault is coming from within.

What's worse, the assault on our schools and our children's future is one we, the people, have allowed to happen and seem powerless to resist. We are referring to the barrage of standardized testing besetting our schools and districts. No Child Left Behind is only its most recent, and most punishing, incarnation. And the Obama administration's proposals for "amending" NCLB reflect a similarly misguided reliance on test scores as the primary measures of success for students, teachers, and the education system as a whole. For decades more and more tests have been seeping into our schools, sapping the energy and enthusiasm of educators and draining the life from children's learning. And while some of the motivation for this burgeoning movement is clearly commercial, it is at least partly driven by what we have come to think of as "the tyranny of good intentions."

Those are some pretty dire charges, but we argue that, because of the way we insist on using these tests, they damage society in ways that far outweigh the minimal benefits they confer—whether the tests are used for "measuring achievement" in the K–12 schools or for helping to determine admission to college. We hope to persuade you that you need to look beyond the good intentions expressed by those who continue to support this plague of tests, and we plan to arm you with some basic understanding of standardized tests and the assumptions—almost never discussed in public forums—that underlie them. As the title of our book suggests, these assumptions are largely mythical. Like myths, they embody a system of beliefs that characterize a particular culture. But unlike myths, we use the assumptions that underlie standardized tests to make policies and drive practices that influence the lives of our children and so greatly affect our future.

If you're experiencing serious déjà vu about now, we sympathize. If the thought of reading still more complicated and confusing information about standardized testing—including all those arcane details about margins of sampling error and reliability coefficients—makes you want to run screaming from the room, take it from us, we're right behind you. So why, then, have we subjected ourselves to the prolonged project of creating this book, and why do we hope that you'll agree that the time you give it is time well spent?

The answer lies in that very sense of déjà vu. We have all heard the complaints about standardized testing before. Walter Lippmann was among the first to make them—in the 1920s. And Banesh Hoffmann, back in 1962, raised serious questions in *The Tyranny of Testing* about what standardized tests could really tell us about the achievement or the aptitude of our youngsters. (This book has been reissued in paperback, by the way, and is available on Amazon.com and other websites.) More recent critiques have come from Peter Sacks, Alfie Kohn, W. James Popham, Daniel Koretz, Gerald Bracey, and many other commentators and researchers, all sounding off on the proper role of testing in America. They've warned us of the distortions that inevitably arise when we ignore the capabilities of our technologies. And they've told us that many of the test-based inferences that politicians and pundits routinely draw about American schools and children are unsound. In addition, FairTest and its Assessment Reform Network, along with other groups devoted to the rational use of tests, work hard every day to make the limitations of standardized tests clear.

So haven't we heard such criticism often enough? Maybe not. Look at that list of names in the preceding paragraph. How many do you recognize? We're betting that most readers will be unfamiliar with nearly all of them, and we think that, as educators, parents, and concerned citizens, you will want to learn more about them and their work. If the messages these commentators have been sending for decades had been received and digested by the public, we wouldn't be asking you to spend a few hours with us and think this problem through. We would all have moved on to the myriad other problems that confront schools and educators every day, problems that won't be fixed by another truckload of test scores.

But though the messages have been sent, they haven't gotten through. The repeated remarks of America's opinion leaders make this fact painfully clear. For example, Peter Wood is executive director of the National Association of Scholars, an organization of conservative academics. Presumably, he's smart enough to recognize nonsense when he hears it—nonsense like the negative characterization of U.S. students' performance in science, which Bill Gates derived from the trends of international test scores and offered to the nation's elected leaders. Wood's own argument about the role of American culture in driving students away from the serious study of science may or may not hold water. That's an argument for another book. We quote him here because he accepts unquestioningly Gates's assumption that the trends in scores on international tests are a fair and accurate reflection of math and science education in America. (We take a brief look at what international comparative assessments can be good for in chapter 1; it's not a long section.) Wood summarizes Gates's words without apology or explanation, and presumably with a straight face:

> Our record on high-school math and science education is particularly troubling. International tests indicate that American fourth-graders rank among the top students in the world in science and above average in math. By eighth grade, they have moved closer to the middle of the pack. By 12th grade, our students score near the bottom of all industrialized nations. As a result, too many of them enter college without even the basic skills needed to pursue a degree in science or engineering.[1]

Of course, Bill Gates has *numbers* to back him up. And although we Americans say we hate math—and Gates's comments about poor learning in math and science fall squarely within that cultural comfort zone—we nonetheless love numbers. We treasure them and bring them out for display on special occasions. Batting averages, game-winning RBIs, free-throw percentages, the Dow Jones average. You name it, and if it's got numbers that we can arrange in an ordered list, then we want that list. And if you have numbers over an extended period of time, then we can create trends. We love those trend numbers even more. We want to compare the "home team" with everyone else. We want to know: Who's in the lead? Who's moving up? Who's moving down? And like the seers of days gone by, we use our numbers to try to predict the future.

The Book of Lists was a best seller in the 1970s, and if anything, our national obsession with ranking has only gotten stronger with the arrival on the scene of computers and the World Wide Web. Today, anyone can crunch up some crispy numbers, and everyone can be a list maker. Think of the reports in your local newspaper whenever your state releases test scores for local schools. Do you see the equivalent of a league table? An ordered list of the winners and losers? We thought so. And here in our own university town, each year some faculty members rail against the proliferation of college and department rankings—the one by *U.S. News and World Report* may be the most famous, but it is far from alone. Yet when a list maker rates one of Indiana University's schools or departments in the top ten, that's news—front-page news in the local paper and news for dissemination by the university's public relations staff. Numbers, whatever their provenance, are deemed to measure some underlying reality.

There's little harm in playing around with numbers and lists as long as you understand where the numbers come from and what—if anything—they mean. However, we greatly fear that this understanding is largely missing from today's public discussions of test scores, and we're not at all sure that very much talk about what the scores mean even takes place. And that talk should be taking place all the time, because the outcomes of these tests are being used to determine what your children learn and what opportunities will be open to them.

But most Americans seem to hold views about testing that can best be described as "intuitive," though not necessarily correct. Henry Braun and Robert Mislevy have written about "Intuitive Test Theory," and they liken it to the kind of intuitive beliefs about physics that people adopt as children—and then cling to for the rest of their lives.[2] These are beliefs like "heavy objects fall faster than light ones." Seems to make sense and works well in daily life, except perhaps in physics class. But it's totally wrong. Such ideas work pretty well for navigating the world, but you wouldn't want to base a moon landing on them. While we won't be dealing explicitly with the intuitive ideas cited by Braun and Mislevy, many of the assumptions about standardized testing that we treat are the result of such widely held—and fallacious—beliefs.

We hope that this book will enable you to think less intuitively about tests. We think every concerned citizen ought to be raising serious questions about the standardized tests used in their schools, about the decisions that are based on the outcomes of those tests, and about the potential for harm as a result of those published school "report cards." We hope to enable you to ask questions of the people who are making the decisions—as citizens first, but also as parents and educators yourselves. Talk with your children's teachers and your school's administrators. You might be surprised to find many of them less than comfortable with the current situation. Question your local superintendent, your school board, and your elected officials at the community and state levels. One of our goals is to provide you with enough information and especially with sources of additional information to enable you to ask hard questions—and to follow up on the superficial answers that we fear you will encounter all too often.

Why do we think many of the answers you get from school leaders and politicians are likely to be superficial? During the politically charged month before the 2008 elections, Indiana's candidates for state superintendent of schools took part in a community forum in Bloomington. (Now, we don't intend to pick on Indiana's education leaders any more than on the leaders of other states; we just happen to live here. But we think you'll find the comments of our leaders in line with what you hear where you live.) Both candidates were reasonable and experienced superintendents. However, when the subject of standardized testing came up, their good judgment deserted them. First, they pointed to problems that special education students and those still learning English have with the tests, then they noted that tests provide only "one measure of school success," and finally they expressed a desire to communicate outcomes more clearly to parents—sensible, if not deep, positions. But then the eventual winner of the election argued, unchallenged by his opponent, that testing is here to stay. "That is the mechanism we have. We may not like it."[3]

AN AERIAL VIEW

Every military leader knows it's always valuable to have an aerial view of the terrain to be contested. Before we address the individual assumptions that underlie standardized testing, we look briefly at this "big picture" in chapter 1. That aerial photograph will give you the lay of the land that we'll be traversing together. In chapter 1, we look briefly at the accountability system we've created—mostly in the past twenty-five years—and examine the confusion of purpose that it reflects. We take up recent proposals to improve that accountability system in chapter 10, and we sort out the confusion of purpose that afflicts our schools in chapter 11, concluding that many of the perceived problems of today's schools are better understood and would be better resolved by working to return the schools to their historical purpose: the preparation of the next generation of citizens for our democratic republic.

Finally, in a short concluding section, chapter 1 briefly explores the terra incognita of international assessments of educational achievement. We ask both what they are good for and what they're *not* good for. And we find that, like the unknown territory at the edges of a medieval map, in the land of international assessments, "There be dragons." In short, the international assessments are mostly a distraction for the public and for policy makers and are useful primarily for what professional educators and students of pedagogy might be able to learn from some of the better ones conducted in recent decades, especially those efforts that have sought to go behind the classroom door.

UNQUESTIONED ASSUMPTIONS

But, to paraphrase our state superintendent, if we don't like the mechanism we have, we can change it. We put it in place. Yet in order to see that we can change, we have to stop for a moment and think through what the tests are capable of telling us and what we really want to know. They're not always the same things, and they are things we rarely pause to think about.

Indeed, the idea for this book grew out of discussions we've had over the years about exactly what are the assumptions that underlie standardized testing. Here are some questions that will help you focus on the assumptions we'll be dealing with in some detail in the following chapters. Think back and ask yourself about the many ways most of us never pause to consider what's up with standardized tests:

- Have you ever thought about how well students' knowledge and skills can be assessed by the limited sample of content included in a forty-five-question test? What does a score on that test tell you about the vast range of content that simply can't be included? (See chapter 2.)
- Have you ever talked about the high achievement at a particular school when all you really knew about the school was the average test scores of its students? (See chapter 3.)
- Have you ever argued—or heard someone argue—that what we need is objective information about student achievement? For most people that word *objective* used in a school context automatically means standardized test scores and very little else. (See chapter 4.)
- Have you or your school system ever handed out punishments or rewards to schools, to teachers, or to individual children based on their test scores? How motivational are such practices? (See chapter 5.)
- Have you ever thought that improvement in scores on "high stakes" tests is a sound indicator of improvement in learning? (See chapter 6.)
- Have you ever wondered about whether the tests have an effect on the curriculum and on classroom life? Have you ever questioned what's left out to make time for the tests themselves and for the often extensive preparation for them? (See chapter 7.)
- Have you ever given more weight to an "indirect" measure (a standardized test score) of student achievement than to a "direct" assessment of achievement? Direct assessments range from judgments teachers make

to your own reading of your children's work to the response of those who attend a school performance or a school open house. (See chapter 8.)
- Have you ever thought that moving to a district or attendance area with high test scores would mean high achievement and success in life for your children? How well do standardized tests forecast future success—in school, of course, but also throughout life? (See chapter 9.)

There are literally dozens of other assumptions that all of us—from policy makers to school officials to ordinary citizens—routinely make about standardized tests. We will focus on those that grow out of the questions listed above, but once you start to think this way about the tests, you'll come up with other questions that will reveal other infrequently examined assumptions. If you come up with some other questionable assumptions and you'd like some feedback, feel free to share them at http://thoughtsonstandardized-testing.blogspot.com. We'd be happy to hear what you think, and we think the discussions generated might be both revealing and useful.

Here are a few additional assumptions that we don't deal with in any detail but are surely worth thinking about. The tests are timed. Is faster necessarily better? Better for everything? When your state reports proficiency, what does that mean and who says so? Is answering a question—whether filling in a bubble or writing in a short response—in any way equivalent to finding, posing, and solving a real problem in context? Why do standardized achievement tests assess the particular array of skills that they do? Who decides on that array, and how?

We'll stop here, but you don't have to. Think about what we tacitly assume to be true about the system of assessment that is consuming ever more time in children's school days. And ask yourself if what we're learning from our assessment system is worth the price.

MODUS OPERANDI

We promise this will be our only Latin heading. We pledge not to cave in and go for something close, like "valedictory." This is our shorthand way of saying, "Here's how we're going to address the questions and assumptions we just listed."

We will work in two ways. First, we will appeal to your sense of logic and common sense. However, in the world of assessment, common sense can often deceive us, so we'll also refer you to the experts in the field who will tell you in their own words what's appropriate to assume about tests and what's not. We'll examine the logic of the assumptions underlying standardized testing, draw on the judgments of experts in the field, and relay that information to you, along with our opinion of what it all means for our schools and our children.

From the general tenor of these pages, you won't be surprised to learn that we dispute many of the basic assumptions embodied in the questions we listed above. We don't dispute them because we have some ax to grind where testing is concerned. We were once fans of the tests, and we've included our own personal testing histories—or Testing Autobiographies—as brief interludes throughout the book so that you can form some opinion of what led us to our current position. We hope that seeing how we moved from naive but essentially *pro*-testing positions to where we stand today will persuade you to consider the arguments we make and then to explore some of the sources we cite. If you do so, we believe your testing history will follow a similar path. All of those to whom we showed early drafts of this book automatically began to recall their own experience with standardized tests, and we invite you to reflect on your experience and that of your children and any other individuals whose lives you know well. What role did the testing play in their lives and in the decisions they made?

As our testing autobiographies make clear, we acquired our skepticism about the assumptions from a combination of our own experience and because the large body of psychometric science just does not support them.[4] We didn't conduct this research ourselves, and we are not assessment experts. Instead, we base our judgments on the published works of a number of eminent psychometricians and policy analysts who have examined these issues carefully through the lens of their professional expertise. Sometimes they have conducted original research, and sometimes they have gathered and synthesized the research of others. We find their conclusions persuasive—for statistical and logical reasons and because they mesh well with our own experience. We will quote from these experts liberally, in part to give you the flavor of the conclusions in the authors' own words and in part to persuade you to seek out their published works. If you care about where our schools are headed and about the future of all our children, we encourage you to follow up and seek more information than we have the space or the expertise to give you here. In a sense, we hope that this book will function somewhat like a Web portal: you won't find all the answers you seek here, but you'll find the connections and signposts that will guide your exploration of this complex and socially charged matter.

We've also asked a few people who have a range of experience and expertise in testing and measurement to give us a few brief comments on potential uses for standardized tests. We believe there are some, but we also believe they're not the uses most people are familiar with. We'll include their views in a series of sidebars interspersed throughout the text.

We also do not intend to refight old academic battles. The academic fight over the use of a single test score to determine eligibility for a program or benefit or to impose sanctions or to retain a student in a grade for an additional year has long been concluded. The test-'em-till-they-improve team lost. The three main professional associations that deal with psychometrics—the American Psychological Association, the American Educational Research Association, and the National Council on Measurement in Education—issued a revised set of standards for the use of testing nearly a decade ago.[5] (A panel to revise the standards was appointed in September 2008, but its work is not likely to be done in time for us to make use of it.)

You need to know up front that the standards adopted by these three associations are frequently violated by all manner of programs and policies, some federal, some state, some local. The 1999 version of the standards organized the field of assessment into the broad areas of test construction, fairness, and application. Most of the violations we refer to have taken place in the area of application, where judgments are frequently made about individual children on the basis of tests designed to assess group performance, where children are routinely denied high school diplomas as a result of a test score, where access to special programs for high achievers depends on a test score. If you believe that the leading professional associations and the leading psychometricians and analysts know what they're talking about—and we do believe them—then you'll agree that the way we use tests in public schools needs to change and come into line with the best thinking in psychometrics.

Those who continue to advocate for the misguided uses of standardized tests tend to be policy makers, corporate leaders, and politicians, rather than educators. But the important point is not who they are but that their arguments are not based on sound evidence. They are, in fact, based on equal measures of rhetorical sleight of hand, wishful thinking, and a widespread public faith in the almost magical inerrancy of numbers.

In addressing the underlying assumptions of standardized tests, we'll do more than introduce you to the conclusions of the nation's leading psychometricians. We'll take a few shots of our own. And while we marshal the evidence of the experts in quotations and notes, we will draw on our own understanding of human beings and human societies to address the widespread cultural appeal of the "pro-testers." We acknowledge the attractiveness of simple answers to complex questions, but, like H. L. Mencken, we believe they are highly likely to be wrong.

Just about everyone—politicians, school leaders, teachers, parents, and indeed almost all citizens—has grown up with these tests. They became a part of the background of life in the last half of the twentieth century, and their importance has only intensified in the twenty-first. Standardized testing is to Americans as water is to a fish. We don't even see that things could be different. We hope this book will make it clear just how wet we all are.

A MEDLEY OF VIEWS

A great many people have given the matter of standardized tests and their use a great deal of thought. We asked some of them for brief responses to this question: *Please describe what, in your view, are the appropriate uses of standardized tests in U.S. schools.* In this introduction and at the end of chapters 1, 2, 6, 7, 8, 9, and 10, we present A Medley of Views that we received. Some commentators said that, when certain guidelines are observed, standardized tests can be quite useful; some saw no possibilities whatever for the tests. But no one we asked endorsed the current use of the tests for accountability purposes under No Child Left Behind or the new administration's proposed uses in its "blueprint." We didn't ask Secretary of Education Arne Duncan or his predecessor Margaret Spellings.

Ⓐ Ⓑ Ⓒ Ⓓ

"READING" THE READING TESTS, SUSAN OHANIAN

Early in my teaching career, I thought standardized tests had some minimal use. I thought they let me know if my students, in general, were able to do what experts expected. But the more knowledgeable I became about child development and the closer I looked at the tests, the more I began to suspect the so-called expertise of the test producers. So I tried skewing the results. For example, guessing that test makers would consider apostrophe placement a big deal for third-graders and guessing that they would try to lure kids with sins of commission, before the test I told my students, "You know, we don't use apostrophes in this class, and I'll break the knuckles of anybody who says the right answer is to add an apostrophe."

Predictably, the test had two such items, and my class, grouped together as the worst readers in third grade, obeyed my threat and scored above grade level in Language Arts Usage. I think my method is saner than drilling hapless third-graders all year on the difference between possession and plurality.

They also scored high in spelling even though they were abominable spellers. On standardized tests spelling is really proofreading, and since my students did a *lot* of reading, they were adept at recognizing what "looked" right. Later, it was hard to convince parents that their children really weren't fine spellers when McGraw-Hill claimed they were "above grade level."

Now, as I collect absurd standardized test questions from across the country, my misgivings grow. In testing comprehension, some test makers use vile passages constructed by work-for-hire temps. Others use "authentic" literature, degrading that literature in the process. When I saw the mutilation done to D. B. Johnson's *Henry Hikes to Fitchburg*, I burst into tears. Surely, D. B. Johnson did not create this work so kids will identify an adjective when they see it. The MCAS (Massachusetts Comprehensive Assessment System) asked tenth-graders to read a passage from *The Grapes of Wrath* by John Steinbeck and then answer this question:

The sentence "From her position as healer, her hands had grown sure and cool and quiet; and faultless in judgment as a goddess" begins with

Ⓐ a split infinitive.
Ⓑ an independent clause.
Ⓒ a prepositional phrase.
Ⓓ a gerund phrase.

As though Nobel Laureate writers write to provide children with grammar lessons. Or as if this information has anything to do with reading comprehension.

Test manufacturers would never be able to keep the lid on just how outrageous their reading comprehension tests are if looking at these tests weren't a felony in many states. Teachers and parents and the public aren't allowed to have a clue.

For anyone who administers standardized tests to children or whose children take standardized tests, *Children and Reading Tests* (Hill and Larsen, JAI Press, 2000) is a must-read. Must. No matter what your level of expertise in deciphering reading tests, this book will knock your socks off. Using methods of discourse analysis, the authors examine representative material from actual reading tests, and they discuss children's responses. In short, they talk to children about why they chose the answers they did. In a sophisticated and nuanced revelation we see both how tests fail to tap into children's worldviews and how convincing children's "wrong" answers are.

Susan Ohanian is a teacher and writer who lives in Vermont. She hosts the website www.susanohanian.org, which was founded in opposition to No Child Left Behind.

1

Misunderstanding Accountability: The Big Picture

Schools are not businesses; they are a public good.

—Diane Ravitch, 2010

$\mathbf{W}$e open with the "aerial view" we promised in the Introduction. Before moving on to the specific assumptions that underlie standardized testing and the ways we use it in America, we want to give you the lay of the land as well as a preview of the better place we hope we can end up.

The big questions for our big-picture view are: Why testing, and why now? The short answer to both questions is that today, accountability rules. Everyone knows it. No Child Left Behind brought to a head twenty years of a misguided approach to accountability that has grown progressively more misguided. The model of accountability that our policy makers generally espouse takes an "industrial" approach to schooling. It defines the value of all our educational efforts strictly in terms of test scores and so makes increasing those scores the primary goal of our schools. It's as if our leaders believe that you can gather up a bushel of high test scores—fresh from the academic assembly line—and take them to market and cash them in for future prosperity.

Look at the Race to the Top, the portion of the American Recovery and Reinvestment Act of 2009 (between us, the stimulus bill) that provided more than $4 billion for a grants competition among the states, or look at the early indications of what the administration and Congress are likely to end up with in a reauthorized ESEA (Elementary and Secondary Education Act), spelled out in *A Blueprint for Reform*.[1] We're going to "hold people accountable" by requiring schools to track student outcomes from test scores to attendance to graduation rates. In designing compensation systems, we're going to require states to consider teachers' performance—as measured at least in part by their

13

students' performance on standardized tests. And we're going to have "interventions" for teachers and schools that fail to produce ever-higher numbers. After all, what could schools possibly be for, if they're not for producing ever-higher performance numbers? Many folks in D.C. and in state capitals are even hoping to extend similar kinds of accountability measures to higher education.

But all of this effort is, we contend, misguided for at least two reasons. First, we're caught up in a national misunderstanding of the basic terms of the debate. The proposed policies aren't about *accountability* at all. All school accountability really *ought* to mean is that citizens and their elected officials are given the information that they need to know about their schools. That's far simpler to state than to put into effect. But the information the public needs to have about its schools is far broader and more complex than any set of test scores.

Accountability is really just reporting.[2] And while reporting test scores and other quantitative measures of the performance of schools and students certainly constitutes a part of that task, it is only a small part. What teachers share during parent conferences about how students are progressing is part of accountability; the budget figures presented at school board meetings and reported by local news outlets are important too, and so is the array of demonstrations of student achievement in the arts and in athletics. The aim of accountability is to allow the public to get to know its schools, and transparency is key.

But real communication is a two-way street. Schools also need to invite real public input into matters of curriculum, instruction, extracurricular activities, and all the problems and successes, social and academic, that are part of the daily life of our schools. Then our schools will be truly accountable. In chapter 10, we take a more in-depth look at accountability and examine in some detail two recent proposals for new ways to design an accountability system that is broader and more responsive to the role of public education in a democratic society.

But if the so-called accountability policies being considered by our leaders, both elected and appointed, are not about accountability, what are they about? In a word, they are about *evaluation*, and evaluation means making judgments. Are our students doing well enough and are our teachers good enough to help them? Which brings us to the second reason that the policies under consideration are misguided: judgment requires a broad consideration of purpose, and in our haste to get to the finish line, find out who won, and award the trophies and hand out the lashes, we don't stop and think about why we do what we do. What are our schools for? What goals do we hope they will achieve?

These questions of purpose are not new, and in chapter 11 we look at the long history of thoughtful consideration of the purpose of public schools. But taking them seriously requires patient and nuanced discussion, something that our national rush to judge and then reward or punish on the flimsy foundation of a set of test scores has made all too rare. This book is intended to move you to instigate such discussions with your family, friends, and neighbors. This kind of change that bubbles up from the people is a reassertion of the democratic values on which the nation was founded, and in it lies the kind of reform we believe our schools need.

More than a quarter century after *A Nation at Risk* moved school reform onto the national political stage, more than twenty years after the first President Bush and the nation's governors set "national goals" for education for the year 2000 (heard much about them lately?), and after more than eight long years of the punitive accountability schemes of No Child Left Behind, the time seems ripe to consider these kinds of questions. Indeed, some events suggest that the stars are aligned.

As we were putting the finishing touches on this book, a loud splash was heard in the usually calm pond of education publishing. Diane Ravitch, an education historian who is a research professor at New York University and was from 1991–1993 Assistant Secretary of Education in the George H. W. Bush administration, published a new book. Its title, *The Death and Life of the Great American School System*, harks back to Jane Jacobs's *Death and Life of Great American Cities*. And its impact might turn out to be just as profound.

As a writer and as a federal policy maker, Ravitch was one of the key architects of the standards movement of the 1990s, which had only a short life and was quickly replaced by the extreme emphasis on high-stakes testing that NCLB represented. Her support for the role of choice, charter schools, and markets in education was never in question, and she often wrote in support of these market-based ideas. Her new book is essentially a recanting of nearly all her once stoutly held views about "testing, accountability, choice, and markets." As she repeats throughout the book, *the evidence for these policies just isn't there.*

Of Ravitch's quartet of policies she once endorsed and now disputes, our focus is primarily on the first two: testing and accountability. Our book is devoted to demonstrating the shortcomings of the measuring stick of standardized testing that is so mindlessly used to judge schools, and we're happy to have someone as influential as Ravitch cross over to our side on that one.

But an expressed desire for accountability is at least partly responsible for the test mania that continues to beset the nation. Ravitch describes policy makers' understanding of accountability when No Child Left Behind became law in 2002: "By accountability, elected officials meant that they wanted the schools to measure whether students were learning, and they wanted rewards or punishments for those responsible."[3] It's our view that the rewards and punishments employed to entice or push schools to raise test scores are at best misguided and at worst harmful (see chapter 5 and, to a lesser extent, chapter 6). Indeed, one of the main weaknesses in the Obama "blueprint" is that it maintains the same obsession with the use of carrots and sticks. And while even NCLB didn't use the word *punishment* when referring to the sticks to be applied to schools, preferring "sanctions" instead, the Obama administration's new locution, "interventions," slathers on the rhetoric even thicker. It's not hard to envision such an "intervention" as consisting of a ring of politicians and corporate leaders surrounding a group of tearful teachers and students and haranguing them for being lazy and unmotivated.

But Ravitch does more than simply disavow some of her earlier views and critique the techniques used to seek to drive schools to raise test scores. Like us, she also recognizes the importance of goals and purposes. She writes that "everyone involved in educating children should ask themselves why we educate. What is a well-educated person? What knowledge is of most worth? What do we hope for when we send our children to school?" She accepts as obvious that we want children to learn to read and write, but she goes much further:

> [T]hat is not enough. We want to prepare them for a useful life. We want them to be able to think for themselves when they are out in the world on their own. We want them to have good character and to make sound decisions about their life, their work, and their health. We want them to face life's joys and travails with courage and humor. We hope that they will be kind and compassionate in their dealings with others. We want them to have a sense of justice and fairness. We want them to understand our nation and our world and the challenges we face. We want them to be active, responsible citizens, prepared to think issues through carefully, to listen to differing views, and to reach decisions rationally. We want them to learn science and mathematics so they understand the problems of modern life and participate in finding solutions. We want them to enjoy the rich artistic and cultural heritage of our society and other societies.[4]

And she sees these goals as derived from the essential purpose of schooling in America. As we explain in chapter 11, since the founding of our republic, the purpose of public schooling in America has been to produce fully formed adults, ready to take their place in the democratic society we have passed on to them. Here is Ravitch:

> Our schools will not improve if we expect them to act like private, profit-seeking enterprises. Schools are not businesses; they are a public good. The goal

of education is not to produce higher scores, but to educate children to become responsible people with well-developed minds and good character.[5]

Measuring well-developed minds and good character really is tougher than rocket science, and neither task lends itself well to measurement by a standardized test.

But no matter how we spell out the various goals of schooling, when the discussion ends, schools remain crucial to creating the next generation of citizens. Families, religious bodies, and other social institutions play important roles, but in our society, schools are key players, and coming to an understanding of why we even have public schools is worth the time it takes.

In misunderstanding accountability and in rushing to ill-informed judgment, we seem to have forgotten the primary role of purpose. It's as if we're careering down a highway at breakneck speed, happy just to be in motion. But lacking either a GPS system or a map, we have no idea where we're going.

SATELLITE VIEW

While an aerial view of the landscape of education might take in this nation and the accountability policies that it now follows, to get a picture of the entire world, we need to switch to a satellite view. What are we to make of all those international comparisons? You know, the ones you've heard and read about that purport to show America's students are doing far worse than their counterparts in the rest of the industrialized world. What's more, in many of these analyses it's often alleged that the relative performance of American students declines the longer they stay in school and that we can't expect to have a competitive economy if we don't have competitive students.

Most of what you hear and read on this score is a combination of noise and nonsense. We deal with the matter briefly here because we don't want you to be sidetracked by all the hoopla the next time a new set of comparative test scores is released.

Of course, all of the assumptions that we're about to consider with regard to standardized testing in general also apply to the tests used in international comparisons. (See our list of bulleted questions in the Introduction.) That means that comparative reports, especially when filtered through the consciousness of pundits and politicians, should be taken with an even larger grain of salt. But there are some new complications that are peculiar to international comparisons.

The late Gerald Bracey, who was one of those who contributed brief thoughts on the potential uses of standardized tests that we've interspersed throughout this book, maintained a blog on Huffington Post for a number of years. One of the final entries before his death in the fall of 2009 dealt with nine myths about public schools, one of which was that student test scores are related to the economic competitiveness of a nation:

> We do well on international comparisons of reading, pretty good on one international comparison of math and science, and not so good on another math/ science comparison. But these comparisons are based on the countries' average scores, and average scores don't mean much. The Organisation for Economic Co-operation and Development, the producer of the math/science comparison in which we do worst, has pointed out that in science the U.S. has 25% of all the highest scoring students in the entire world, at least the world as defined by the 60 countries that participate in the tests. Finland might have the highest scores, but that only gives them 2,000 warm bodies compared to the U.S. figure of 67,000. It's the high scorers who are most likely to become leaders and innovators. Only four nations have a higher proportion of researchers per 1,000 full-time employees, Sweden, Finland, New Zealand, and Japan. Only Finland is much above the U.S.[6]

As we argue in chapter 4, averages are capable of obscuring as much as they reveal. And it's clear that no nation's economy can be made up entirely of engineers and scientists, so the entire enterprise of judging an economy by average test scores in math or science or even in reading is really a fruitless exercise. But there are many other reasons that these international comparisons of test scores are not very revealing.

Bracey wrote extensively on this topic. Much of his work was published in the *Phi Delta Kappan*, a magazine for professional educators, as part of his monthly research columns, or in one of the eighteen Bracey Reports that appeared in the magazine between 1991 and 2008.[7]

The first question to ask about the comparisons is how representative of the population of each nation is the sample of students tested. If you go all the way back to the earliest studies in the 1960s, there really were vast differences in the population of students in school. We were comparing pumpkins and kumquats, and pretty much everyone knew it. Many nations were still recovering from the effects of a global war, and not every nation was dedicated to educating all of its citizens.

The most egregious problems with sampling were fixed to some degree when the results of the first International Evaluation of Educational Progress were released in 1989. In the follow-up, in 1991, things were even better. Subsequently, such exams as the various iterations of TIMSS (Third International Mathematics and Science Study) and PISA (Programme for International Student Assessment), running from the 1990s into the 2000s, did an even better job of trying to compare apples to apples.

But it still doesn't work very well. Bracey cites a Belgian analysis of PISA results from 2007 that said:

> [T]he broad and long-term effects of education cannot be reduced to a few trivial indicators and every education system could be validly understood only by taking account of its history, its aims, and the complexity of its structures.[8]

And the matter of structure and purpose of a nation's school system cannot be overemphasized. For example, on the morning after the first round of TIMSS results were released in 1995, Lowell Rose, director of the PDK/Gallup Poll of the Public's Attitudes toward the Public Schools, was chairing a committee meeting to come up with questions for that fall's poll. He wanted to acknowledge the poor performance of U.S. students in the TIMSS data. Other panelists encouraged him to first get the background documents for the study from the researchers at Boston College who were in charge of the U.S. TIMSS effort.

Dr. Rose had strong views, but he was not immune to evidence. When he obtained a copy of the background material and saw wide differences in the structure of the education systems of the nations included, he agreed with other panelists that asking any questions about the results would be less than revealing. Just a few of the anomalies with regard to the secondary school results that purported to measure the performance of those in the final year of schooling: U.S. students worked at paying jobs for more hours than students in any other nation; the calculus portion of the exam included U.S. students who were in precalculus and had taken no calculus at all; students in the final year of schooling ranged in age from seventeen to their early twenties; while only a minority of students in the mid-1990s took even a single high school course in physics, in some nations many students took three; and in other nations, as many as half the students were in vocational programs by age seventeen, and some nations included these students, while others didn't. It was a mess—an interesting mess, perhaps—but a mess nevertheless.

All of the comparisons over the years raise similar questions, so that must mean there's no value in pursuing any kind of international comparison, right? Not exactly. If you want competition, we have the Olympic Games and the World Cup. But one big question school comparisons can help answer is "figur[ing] out which practices from other countries we could use as guides for our own."[9] And some of the studies have provided vast stores of information that you've probably not seen reported in your local newspapers or heard about from your elected representatives.

Consider the TIMSS Video Study, which was first reported in 1995, with a follow-up in 1999.[10] In the first portion of the study, representative samples of eighth-grade math teachers in Japan, Germany, and the United States were videotaped; in the follow-up, samples of teachers in seven nations were taped. The tapes were coded, analyzed, and studied by research teams to shed light on how teachers approached mathematical topics in the various countries and whether those differences were reflected in the test scores. But the greatest value of the TIMSS Video Study is that teachers in every nation can learn—not about practices to adopt wholesale—but about patterns in the classroom practices of their international peers that can inform their own teaching.

The teachers and students, not the test scores, are the stars of these analyses. But the overall conclusion the researchers reached was that there was no obvious way to choose a "best method" of teaching specific topics in mathematics. So even this "best use" of the data gathered as part of an international comparison can't be reduced to headline copy.

So with our big picture in full view, let's begin our closer look at the basic assumptions that underlie standardized testing. In the next chapter we address content sampling, an issue much less widely discussed than the more familiar population sampling.

Ⓐ Ⓑ Ⓒ Ⓓ
MISUNDERSTOOD MEASUREMENT MALLETS,
W. JAMES POPHAM

During the past two decades, American teachers have been constantly clobbered in an effort to get those teachers to "raise students' test scores." With few exceptions, the tests on which those scores are to be raised are standardized achievement tests. Such tests, because they are being employed to hold educators accountable for the effectiveness of their instruction—have come to be known as *educational accountability tests*. It is these accountability tests that serve as the measurement mallets by which legislators and policy makers hope to pound teachers into doing a better job of teaching. Nearly everyone involved in the accountability fray thinks standardized, educational accountability tests are the right tools to be used when determining the quality of schooling. They are wrong.

Here's why. In order for a test to provide accurate evidence by which to judge the caliber of instruction given to students, the test must be able to distinguish between students who have been well taught and students who have not. Putting it more technically, a suitable accountability test needs to be *instructionally sensitive*; that is, it must accurately reflect the quality of instruction specifically provided to promote students' mastery of what is being assessed. Almost all of the accountability tests currently being used in this country are instructionally *insensitive*. They simply don't give us accurate evidence by which to judge our schools.

When the accountability tests being used to judge the quality of teaching provide misleading data, they lead to erroneous decisions about schools and end up eroding educational quality. Thus, because of these instructionally insensitive accountability tests, instructionally *effective* schools may be regarded as ineffective and made to scrap their excellent instructional activities. Conversely, instructionally *ineffective* schools may be thought to be effective and encouraged to continue their seemingly fine but actually lame instructional practices.

One reason many of today's accountability tests do such a dismal job in determining educational quality is that those tests were built according to a traditional test-construction approach—an approach intended chiefly to permit fine-grained comparisons among test takers. The desire for a comparative interpretation requires that students' test scores be sufficiently spread out. This requirement means that almost all of the items on a test must contribute meaningfully to the "score-spread" that's necessary to support comparative interpretations.

One of the best ways to get test items to produce score-spread is to make sure students' performances on the items are influenced by background factors that, themselves, are nicely spread out. For example, students' socioeconomic status (SES) is a nicely spread-out variable. So too are students' inherited academic aptitudes, such as their quantitative or verbal aptitudes. Accordingly, if a test item is closely linked to either SES or inherited aptitudes, students' scores on the variable will be spread out as well. And here's where the real problem arises: instructionally insensitive accountability tests tend to measure *what students bring to school*, rather than what they are taught once they get there.

As long as we continue to evaluate schools by using instructionally insensitive accountability tests, our appraisal of those schools will be seriously flawed.

W. James Popham is an emeritus professor at the University of California, Los Angeles. He is the author of a number of works on assessment, including Transformative Assessment *(Association for Supervision and Curriculum Development, 2008).*

2

The Tests Are Too Narrow

Test scores reflect a small sample of behavior and are valuable only insofar as they support conclusions about the larger domains of interest.

—Daniel Koretz, 2008

We begin our look at basic assumptions with the idea of *sampling*. All the assumptions that we take up in subsequent chapters—from the assumption that test scores equal student achievement to the assumption that test scores predict success in life—depend on the central idea that a small portion of a student's behavior fairly represents the whole range of possible behavior.

You've no doubt heard the word most often in reference to "sampling" error.[1] Used in this way, it refers to the drawing of a statistically representative sample of a population to be surveyed—American voters, stay-at-home moms, Florida fourth-graders. The margin of sampling error constrains what we can say about our results. In this chapter, we're referring to *content* sampling, the selection of knowledge and behaviors to be tested in a given assessment from the wide range of knowledge and behaviors that make up the entire domain that we want to know about. There are some general similarities between the two activities, but it's the special nature of content sampling that we want to focus on here.

And don't let the terms *behaviors* and *domain* put you off. Here's a very common experience—that involves both a paper-and-pencil test and a performance test—that should help clarify some terms. Think about your state's driving test. If your state is like Indiana, and it probably is, then you'll first have to pass a written test. In Indiana, that test has thirty-four multiple-choice questions to answer and sixteen road signs to identify. You can miss six questions and fail to identify two signs and still pass, so you need to earn a score of about 83 percent on the questions and 87.5 percent on the road sign identifications.

All of the questions can be answered by information in the state's *Driver's Manual*, which means that the content of the manual is the "domain" of knowledge to be assessed. The specific thirty-four items on a given form of the test are the particular sample chosen to represent that domain, presumably because the items are deemed to represent important areas of the domain, such as how to pass on two-lane roads, what a flashing yellow light means, and what you must hand over to the police officer who stops you if you happen to forget one of the other thirty-three items. Each separate form of the test is a different sample of knowledge drawn from the larger domain.

On the matter of "behaviors," things are only a bit more complicated. While it's true that answering any question—even identifying a railroad crossing sign or selecting a multiple-choice answer—is a behavior as far as psychologists are concerned, most of the rest of us reserve the term to describe something a little larger and more considered. The road test that follows a successful paper-and-pencil test would surely qualify. The examining officer asks you to drive around as you normally would and then gives specific instructions to make left or right turns, sometimes at signals and sometimes not, and, most distressing for a lot of kids these days, to parallel park. The examiner keeps a score sheet and rates your performance. In some ways the scoring is a judgment call, but there are guidelines, such as having both wheels within a certain minimum distance from the curb when you park.

While the standardized tests used in schools are not tests of performance in the same way that the driving test is, there are some aspects that are similar. For example, states sometimes ask students to solve word problems and record the way they set up and carry out their work. In Indiana's math tests, for example, the *answer* to problems such as these—the rightness or wrongness—isn't what's scored. Such questions are considered process questions, and the scoring is done according to a rubric, which is essentially a series of descriptions spelling out what constitutes success and describing the features of more and less successful efforts. So in this way, process questions are not entirely unlike the road test. But one thing that is *always* the same about a math test and a road test is that the behavior sampled is intended to represent a larger domain of performance. There's no way to examine all possible mathematical problems involving, say, a geometric concept like area, any more than you could examine all possible driving situations, from passing an

Amish horse and buggy in rural Knox County, Indiana, to merging into the traffic on I-70 in Indianapolis.

And so, the underlying assumption about standardized testing that we're taking up in this chapter can be stated: *We can select a sample of the knowledge we want kids to learn that accurately represents the entire domain of knowledge we want them acquire.* Surely, this much should at least be possible. After all, every teacher takes a homemade "sample" in an end-of-unit test. If a high school history teacher is making up a test after a unit on the build-up to the Civil War, she'll have to decide how many questions (and what kind of questions, which is another matter) to devote to the Missouri Compromise, how many to the impact of the abolitionist press, and how many to the Dred Scott decision. Fair enough. She knows what she taught and why. She knows what's important in the unit and what she hopes students take away from it. The sample of questions she chooses is directly related to the content she taught.

But a large-scale, standardized achievement test in a particular domain of learning is different, in part because the domain is much wider and so the choice of a representative sample of the content becomes much more difficult. Let's look at an example.

Take the state mathematics standards for fourth grade in Indiana. We're not picking on our home state, but Indiana has been praised for its standards by such groups as the Thomas B. Fordham Foundation, and the state recently unveiled a new website that we wanted to explore. The new site lets a user initiate a search of the state standards by selecting science, math, English, or social studies and specifying a grade level. But before we clicked, we noted that a drop-down menu of choices in addition to the four basic disciplines was available. It offered nineteen other choices and included four areas in the fine arts as well as fifteen other choices where state standards can be found in subjects ranging from agriculture to information literacy. (Another similar menu was available that allowed a user to select standards by elementary grade level.) But the main optional menu yielded a list of nineteen items that included the high school grade levels as well as some specific subjects, such as half-a-dozen special areas in mathematics. For our purposes, though, we chose to stick with a close look at fourth-grade math standards.

And what did we find? There were seven large topic areas: number sense, computation, algebra and functions, geometry, measurement, data analysis and probability, and problem solving. That's like a map of the territory to be covered in fourth-grade math classrooms in Indiana. But it's not very fine-grained. Let's look at one area in more detail. Take computation, an area that's more accessible to people who have been away from math for a time. (How many of us remember very much about algebra and functions?) Here's the statement of the standard for computation:

Students solve problems involving addition, subtraction, multiplication and division of whole numbers and understand the relationships among these operations. They extend their use and understanding of whole numbers to the addition and subtraction of simple fractions and decimals.

Zooming in a little closer, we find a dozen more standards catalogued under this main computation standard. We chose one of these twelve—"add and subtract simple fractions and decimals, using objects or pictures"—and followed the link to "view resources," where we found three items: one a classroom unit and two dubbed "classroom assessments."[2] In this case, the assessments consisted of four separate questions. We don't intend to critique the questions here, just to count them. Under one of the other computational subtopics, we found a classroom assessment with ten such questions, and under others, we found three sets of classroom assessments instead of two.

Let's just assume that each of these twelve subtopics has only two sets of assessments with four questions each (clearly, a lowball estimate). Using our own fourth-grade computational skills (12 x 2 x 4), we make that ninety-six items shown as examples, and that's just for computation. And remember that computation is just one of six large topic areas for fourth-grade math. So there are at least five hundred suggested classroom assessment items presented for fourth-grade math on the Indiana Department of Education website.

Our point is a simple one. Looking just at the subtopics—not the five hundred+ individual assessment items presented—we find that there are fifty-eight subtopics in the Indiana standards of learning for fourth-grade mathematics. If we wish to "cover" each of them and give students a fair chance to show what they know, it's obvious that we should be asking more than one question about each subtopic.

For example, one of the computational subtopics for Indiana fourth-graders has to do with knowing the multiplication tables up through the 10s. While we can probably all agree that we don't need to assess every single multiplication fact, we do need more than a single question to give students a fair chance to show what they know. Of course, they'll also show what they don't know by the mistakes they make, but if we ask only one question in this topic area, we'll have no way of knowing if a student who answers incorrectly a question involving 7 x 8 also doesn't know 7 x 6. You need a fairly large sample of even this very restricted domain if the inferences you're to draw from this test are to be valid.

We'll talk more about test scores and inferences in the next chapter, but an analogy might help here to put the idea of sampling into an everyday context and give a preview of just how complicated drawing inferences from apparently simple data can be. Think about looking out just one window of your home or office. What you see is a sample of the sky, and you notice that it's gray and overcast. That's akin to your test score. It's basic empirical data. But what does that view tell you? First, you need to know that you have a good sample. That is, if you examined other parts of the domain—say, by looking out another window—would the sky still be overcast? If you're looking to the east, but the sky to the west turns out to be clear, there's a problem with your eastward-looking sample. You'll need to account for that sampling problem when you decide whether to look for your rain boots and umbrella.

But suppose you find the sky to be uniformly overcast. What might you infer from your window viewing? That it might rain? That it might snow? That you really don't have enough information to decide? In short, to make a good inference about the weather from the sample you can see, you need to bring more information to the table. If you live in the Midwest and your home is at 68° Fahrenheit, in order to properly interpret that cloudy sky, you'll need to know whether it's June or January. Only then can you decide whether to get out the snow shovel or be on the alert for the tornado sirens.

FACING SOME LIMITS

And that brings us squarely to three other issues of content sampling that present serious problems for those who would use the scores on standardized tests as the primary means of judging the success or failure of students, teachers, and schools. And all three involve limits. The first has to do with setting the boundaries or limits of the domain; the second concerns which items to choose, the luck of the draw you might say; the third takes account of how many items there will be time for.

Setting Boundaries

First, setting the boundaries for a domain of knowledge is not simple. After you separate the math from the English, how do you spread the many topics in either discipline throughout the levels of a school system? Clearly, it depends on what is deemed appropriate for students at a particular grade level, which means it's connected to what someone, somewhere deemed appropriate for students of a certain age or developmental level. Moreover, all of the parts are to some extent interconnected. If you teach two-digit multiplication in fourth grade, you will certainly continue to assess for mastery at higher grade levels. But why are some things taught at one level and not another?

The answer is, we don't really know. A few years back, Weldon Zenger and Sharon Zenger, who were then associated with Kansas State University, published a summary of their fifteen-year effort to answer the question their title posed, "Why Teach Certain Materials at Specific Grade Levels?" Here's how they began an article:

> No solid basis exists in the research literature for the ways we currently develop, place, and align educational standards in school curricula. If this sounds shocking, it should not. The same holds true for placing subject-matter content at specific grade levels (scope and sequence). Basic content criteria or specific subject-matter criteria, for the most part, are not being used to assign content to grade levels. Nevertheless, standards and assessments have come to dominate K-12 curriculum design at national, state, and local levels. And most of these standards come with required assessments that essentially make them mandatory for local school districts.[3]

The Zengers asked readers of the *Phi Delta Kappan*—a professional education journal whose readers include many practicing educators—to help by sending them information regarding "standards and their development, placement, and alignment in the K–12 curriculum." They received very few responses to their request, and the replies they did get most often agreed with the contention that there just wasn't any rhyme or reason to the whole process of putting particular learning at specific grade levels.

The Zengers' findings suggest that the boundaries of the domain to be assessed are, to some degree at least, arbitrary. But every state has its standards documents, which typically give such specific directions as students will "extend their use and understanding of whole numbers to the addition and subtraction of simple fractions and decimals." Since these documents exist, though, shouldn't it be a simple matter to sample the domains they define?

Choosing Items

Well, we wouldn't call it simple, exactly. Harvard's Daniel Koretz spells out clearly what he dubs "the sampling principle of testing": "Test scores reflect a small sample of behavior and are valuable only insofar as they support conclusions about the larger domains of interest."[4] But how to pick items that fairly represent the domain of interest? If you chose items that are too easy, nearly everyone gets them right. If the items are too hard, nearly everyone gets them wrong. Either way, you haven't learned a great deal. So test makers shoot for something in between, a selection of items that will "spread out" the scores of the test takers. Psychometrician James Popham puts it this way:

> To create sufficient score-spread on a traditional standardized achievement test, roughly half of the test-takers should be able to answer the vast majority of the

test's items correctly. The percentage of students who answer an item correctly is referred to as the item's p-value. Thus, an item answered correctly by 50% of students would have a p-value of 0.50. Statistically speaking, items that are the best contributors to a test's overall score-spread are those that have p-values between 0.40 and 0.60.[5]

Think about what this means for a minute. Test makers try out their questions on groups of students. They don't choose items that too many students get wrong, because that doesn't tell us much, except that a few really bright and hard-working students can answer questions that flummox almost all of their peers. And they don't choose items that nearly all the students get right ... why, again? Because that means that almost all the students have actually learned the material tested. But isn't that a good thing? Ordinarily, yes. But it doesn't give those who employ the test—usually policy makers—the kind of information they want. It doesn't spread out the scores; it doesn't identify winners and losers.

The decision to spread the scores by choosing items that roughly half the students will get wrong raises serious questions about how inferences about test scores are used to make decisions about individual schools, teachers, and students. We'll be taking up some of the many issues this practice presents in subsequent chapters. With regard to sampling, though—especially if the scores on a test are to have important consequences for students—it brings up another vexing problem: the luck of the draw. If half the students will answer an item incorrectly, we feel compelled to ask, would a different selection of items with p-values of roughly 0.50 yield different outcomes? Indeed, it would. If enough students are tested, the overall outcomes on different versions of a test should even out and be about the same. But any one person could go from being proficient to needing remediation solely according to the version of the test taken, in other words, the luck of the draw. This selection of items is one of the main sources of measurement error (see glossary for a definition).

Timing and Tests

This brings us to the final sampling issue that poses serious problems for the use of standardized tests to measure the performance of schools, teachers, and students. And that issue is time. There are two time-related issues we want to touch on here: timed tests and students' attention spans.

Since we've just finished a brief discussion of score spread, let's ask how we might take an item that 80 percent of students get right and see to it that only about 50 percent of them succeed. One surefire way is to reduce the amount of time allowed for students to complete a test. Doing that will mean that students will have to speed up and so will be less likely to give a correct answer to any individual item—even if they might have arrived at the correct answer if they had more time.

A timed test has the further drawback of giving students the impression that life, like a TV quiz show, rewards the one who "rings in" first with the correct answer. There are some things in life where making quick decisions is paramount—NFL quarterbacks facing the prospect of a blitz, for example. But in most of our lives, spending an extra moment to reflect before we decide on a course of action will be rewarded. Not on most standardized tests. And of course, many people (and that includes children) don't respond well to such pressures. Thus timed tests are a major source of test anxiety, which education writer Alfie Kohn told us nearly a decade ago has "grown into a subfield of educational psychology." Indeed, Kohn minced no words when he warned us simply, "Beware of tests that are timed."[6]

The second time-related issue is the matter of attention span. Clearly, how large a sample of a domain you can use depends on how long a student being tested can sit still and attend to the task at hand. How long a child is asked to sit still and focus on a test severely constrains the length of that test. And that means that the breadth of the domain that a test can sample is also constrained.

Let's return to Indiana fourth-graders again. Now the folks who make up our state test and the tests used in other states are aware that most kids can't focus on a paper-and-pencil exercise or exam for an extremely long time at a single sitting. So they break up the tests and spread out the testing. The fourth-grade achievement tests in Indiana consist of 115 items that cover both math and reading and include both multiple-choice items and open-ended items. The total time allotted is 415 minutes—nearly seven hours—spread out over three days. Individual districts have the option of spreading out the testing over four days, but they still must give the tests in the specified order.[7] So we're talking about over two hours of testing for several days running. And these hours don't include busy work like passing out the tests, reading through the directions, and collecting the completed answer sheets.

Now there's a popular rule of thumb that says you can estimate the range of normal attention span by multiplying the years a person (*a very young person*) has been alive by 3 and 5. (Don't try this with adults; it doesn't even come close to working!) For our nine-year-old Hoosiers, who are still pretty young, that works out to somewhere between twenty-seven and forty-five minutes. At the higher end, the actual time spent on the test doesn't seem wildly out of range, but there have to be real breaks between parts of the test. Of course, as we all know, people of any age can focus much longer on a task that's freely chosen than on an assigned one. Our own kids sure did. But we don't think many nine-year-olds—or their parents—would find the ISTEP+

so fascinating that they would freely choose to devote some seven hours out of their week to it.

But whether estimates of attention span such as these are precise isn't the issue. The take-away message from this chapter is that you just can't ask children to answer as many questions as you might like to if you really want to cover all of the fifty-eight subtopics in mathematics that Indiana fourth-graders are supposed to have learned. And remember—as in the example we cited about the multiplication tables—to be sure an individual is being judged fairly, you'll need to ask more than one question for each subtopic. Even if you spread out the standardized testing over four days, you still have only 115 questions with which to assess math and reading. And you've got fifty-eight subtopics in math alone. Clearly, some topics are just going to have to be skipped.

We don't have any problem with skipping some of these subtopics on the tests. After all, that's sampling and that's what this chapter is all about. But the necessity of choosing only a sample of the domain you want to know about limits the usefulness of all the standardized tests we use—whether they consist of multiple-choice items or of short-answer items or of essays. We want everyone who has a stake in the education of our children—parents, teachers, policy makers, and elected leaders—to understand these limitations and to stop asking the tests to do what they really can't do. And one reason they can't give you a complete and fair picture of the performance of schools, teachers, and individual children is sampling.

In the next chapter, we'll look at what that incomplete picture is supposed to represent: student achievement. We'll look at what we mean when we say "achievement," and we'll ask how well the standardized tests we use measure that meaning.

A USE OF TESTS I COULD SUPPORT, GERALD W. BRACEY

Existing standardized tests tell us very little. Whether they are high, average, or low, the scores themselves provide no clues as to why they are the way they are. In addition, they are affected by a variety of out-of-school variables ranging from the mother's prenatal care and prenatal ingestion of drugs to lead poisoning and what enrichment experiences are available to children during the summer.

Standardized tests are also insensitive to instruction and seldom provide any diagnostic clues. In medicine, a thermometer shows you if you do or do not have a fever, but other tests must follow to diagnose the cause. Standardized tests don't even work as a thermometer because a student's "temperature" is determined by the kind of outside factors cited above.

During the Eight-Year Study in the 1930s, many standardized tests were developed whose principal function was to provide information to teachers about student needs. They were designed to help a teacher decide what she needed to do next. *Instructionally sensitive* tests is a phrase of recent origin, but one that applies to the tests used in the Eight-Year Study. Today's tests are mostly insensitive to instruction, although the scores can be raised in a variety of ways that don't actually reflect improved instruction. In other words, the system can be gamed. If we could develop instructionally sensitive tests that reflected what teachers were trying to accomplish in the classroom, that would be a use of tests that I could support.

Gerald W. Bracey, an independent writer and researcher who specialized in assessment and policy issues, died in late 2009, shortly after he sent these remarks. Widely known for the Bracey Reports, which appeared annually in the Phi Delta Kappan *from 1991–2008, he was the author of numerous books, mostly recently* Education Hell: Rhetoric vs. Reality *(Educational Research Service, 2009).*

3

The Tests Don't Measure Achievement Adequately

> Measurement of student achievement is complex—too complex for the social science methods presently available.
>
> —Richard Rothstein, 1998

If you were thinking between the lines of the previous chapter, you might have seen this one coming. But even if you didn't anticipate it, we think you'll be ready for it after considering the issue of sampling in some detail. Despite what reports in your local newspaper suggest, scores of standardized tests are *not* the same as student achievement. What's more, the scores don't provide very much useful information for evaluating a student's achievement, a teacher's competency, or the success of a particular school or program. To make such judgments, you need to move beyond the scores themselves and make some inferences about what they might mean.

In this chapter, we'll examine the inferences typically made on the basis of standardized test scores. We'll look at what they show us and what we would really like to know about students, teachers, and schools.

The assumption underlying standardized testing that we're exploring in this chapter is: *When we want to understand student achievement, it is enough to talk about scores on standardized tests.* Accepting this assumption at face value, as nearly all journalists, pundits, and politicians do, is to fall prey to a "dangerous illusion."

INFERENCES ABOUT STUDENTS

Let's start with the question of defining achievement. If someone asked you to say in your own words exactly what is meant by "student achievement," how would you respond? If you said student achievement is what's measured by the state achievement tests, it's time to look a little harder at what these tests actually can and cannot do. More than a decade ago, education economist Richard Rothstein stated the problem directly: "Measurement of student achievement is complex—too complex for the social science methods presently available."[1] And those methods certainly included standardized testing.

That was 1998, but the passage of more than a decade hasn't made it easier to evaluate student achievement in any systematic way, especially in a way that will yield the kind of numbers you can spread out along an axis to make comparisons. If anything, the intervening years—primarily the years of No Child Left Behind (NCLB) and its strict test-driven regimen—have made the problems in this area worse because we've asked test scores to carry ever more weight and we've depended on them to make ever more consequential decisions. Because of NCLB—and the Obama administration's "blueprint" places similar weight on test scores—we now use "achievement test" scores to decide whether students are entitled to tutoring services or whether they can transfer to a different school or whether we should close a school and re-constitute its staff.[2] And many states now have strict rules about who qualifies to receive a high school diploma primarily by the scores on a standardized test of "achievement."

But "achievement" means more than a score on a standardized test. We knew it in 1998, and we know it now. For instance, as part of a larger project to ensure equity in math classrooms, the National Council of Teachers of Mathematics (NCTM), a group whose members are not strangers to the use of numerical data and statistical interpretation, reminded its members of some terms and definitions that would be important in the larger equity project. Rochelle Gutiérrez and her colleagues offered readers of the *NCTM News Bulletin* the following description of an appropriate understanding of "achievement": "Achievement—all the outcomes that students and teachers attain. Achievement is more than test scores but also includes class participation, students' course-taking patterns, and teachers' professional development patterns."[3] The standardized tests we all know so well don't even come close to assessing all the outcomes that students and teachers attain.

As psychometrician Daniel Koretz puts it, scores on a standardized test "usually do not provide a direct and complete measure of educational achievement."[4] He cites two reasons why this is so, and both are related to our earlier discussion of sampling. First, tests can measure only a portion of the *goals* of education, which are necessarily broader and more inclusive than the test could possibly be. We'll be talking in more detail about these broader goals in our final chapter, but it might help to start thinking about them now. Here is Gerald Bracey's list of some of the biggies that we generally don't even try to use standardized tests to measure:

creativity	self-discipline
critical thinking	leadership
resilience	civic-mindedness
motivation	courage
persistence	compassion
curiosity	resourcefulness
endurance	sense of beauty
reliability	sense of wonder
enthusiasm	honesty
empathy	integrity
self-awareness[5]	

Surely these are attributes we all want our children to acquire in some degree. And while not all learning takes place in classrooms, these are real and valuable "achievements." Shouldn't schools pursue goals such as these for their students, along with the usual academic goals? Of course, a teacher can't really teach all of these things from a textbook. But, as Bracey points out, she can model them or talk with students about people who exemplify them. But she has to have enough time left over to do so after getting the kids ready for the standardized test of "achievement."

In fact, there are more problems associated with the impact of standardized testing on "achievement" than simply the fact that the technology of the testing cannot efficiently and accurately measure some vitally important attributes that we all want our children to "achieve." Alfie Kohn put it this way:

> Studies of students of different ages have found *a statistical association between students with high scores on standardized tests and relatively shallow thinking.* One of these studies classified elementary school students as "actively" engaged if they went back over things they didn't understand, asked questions of themselves as they read, and tried to connect what they were doing to what they had already learned; and as "superficially" engaged if they just copied down answers, guessed a lot, and skipped the hard parts. It turned out that the superficial style was positively correlated with high scores on the Comprehensive Test of Basic Skills (CTBS) and Metropolitan Achievement Test (MAT). Similar findings have emerged from studies of middle school and high school students.[6] (Emphasis in original.)

So by ignoring attributes that they can't properly assess, standardized tests inadvertently create incentives for students to become superficial thinkers—to seek the quick, easy, and obvious answer. That's hardly an "achievement" that most parents want for their children. And surely it's not what our policy makers and education officials hope to achieve by incessantly harping on "achievement." In our view, most of these policy makers mean well, but when they say "achievement," they clearly mean test scores and only test scores. But to assume that the test scores can take the place of all the other information we need to know in order to have a good understanding of students' development leads us to some poor conclusions about how our children are growing physically, emotionally, and intellectually. The information provided by test scores is very limited, and consequently we must be very careful in drawing inferences about what the scores mean.

The second reason Koretz cites for the incompleteness of test scores as a measure of achievement directly echoes our discussion of sampling in chapter 2, even in the language he uses: "Even in assessing the goals that can be measured well, tests are generally very small samples of behavior that we use to make estimates of students' mastery of very large domains of knowledge and skill."[7] So apart from not doing a very good job of measuring achievement in such areas as creativity or persistence, standardized tests have another serious limitation: whenever a small part of a domain is made to stand in for the larger whole, we must be very careful about the inferences we draw from the data we obtain.

Another confounding factor when we talk about "achievement" has to do with our casual, everyday use of language. Often, even researchers and academics who know better use the term *achievement* somewhat loosely. We're all guilty of employing such educational shorthand as using a term like *achievement gap* between white and minority students when what we really ought to say is "test-score gap." No doubt we've all heard about this gap, and it is surely troubling. But especially in an area that is so sensitive in our society, we should choose our words carefully and with an eye to accuracy.

What difference does such language use make? When we refer to the gap in terms of "test scores," we remind ourselves of the entire tortured history of the differential impact of standardized testing on social groups in the United States. And that history is more extensive than just the matter of racially or culturally distorted inferences that we might draw from scores on a test—in other words, the biased conclusions we might arrive at. Testing companies and public agencies work to minimize the likelihood that blatant bias of that kind will occur, and they have been reasonably successful in recent years.

But there are other influences on test scores that are not so simply dealt with. Substituting "test-score gap" for "achievement gap" focuses attention on the apparatus of testing, a mechanism that produces data about student performance on a particular set of items so that educators and others can draw inferences about what that performance means. When we think about *score* differences rather than *achievement* differences, we can more easily remember that even well-designed test items will yield different scores according to the level of household income, level of parents' education, the stability of students' living arrangements, and so on. Moreover, these external influences are beyond the control of the students or teachers, and there is a fundamental unfairness in glossing over this fact. Stephen Jay Gould saw the problem clearly with regard to IQ tests, but it applies equally well to any assessment that tries to capture a life in a number and hide a social problem behind a veneer of "science":

> We pass through this world but once. Few tragedies can be more extensive than the stunting of life, few injustices deeper than the denial of an opportunity to strive or even to hope, by a limit imposed from without, but falsely identified as lying within.[8]

In other words, let us resist the temptation to put the burden of solving all the problems of society on the students and teachers in our schools.

Being careful about our language will help us to understand test scores in context. In turn, this more nuanced understanding can guide us toward adopting policies that can help improve our schools and our students' learning, rather than just their test scores.

Using the term *achievement* directs our attention away from the technology of testing and toward the human beings tested. It suggests that we have measured some quality inherent in the students, and our interpretations are likely to reflect such thinking as well. Humans find it very easy to make connections and draw inferences that are simply not supported by a careful examination of the full range of explanations. Construing test scores as stand-ins for "achievement" leads us to adopt the psychometric equivalent of tunnel vision. In the hope of improving the total "outcomes that all teachers and students attain," we focus obsessively on just a single outcome—test scores—to the detriment of effective teaching and learning and program evaluation. So we encourage everyone to use the term *test score* if that's what you really mean. Achievement is something far broader.

Here's an example to help you think about how looking at a too-narrow slice of information can lead to erroneous conclusions. Immediately after World War II, Americans were deemed to be the tallest people in the world; the Japanese were among of the shortest; those in most Western European nations trailed the Americans, but not by much. It wasn't uncommon to hear Americans discussing the inherently small stature of the Japanese. It seemed apparent to Americans that the difference was racial and thus hereditary. If we had had the terminology at the time, we would have inferred from this source of data that the differences were primarily genetic. After all, the white folks—whichever side of the Atlantic they lived on—just seemed to be taller than the Japanese, indeed, taller than most Asians. These were facts, we thought, and we had the numbers to back us up.

Today, all of that has changed. In 2004, *The Guardian* reported on work by John Komlos of Munich University that demonstrated that the Dutch had surpassed the Americans in average height by almost two inches. The Dutch average was nearly 6 feet 2 inches. Even British males had an average height of roughly one-half an inch taller than their American counterparts.[9] Meanwhile, *Guangzhou Daily* reported on the rising height of the Japanese since the 1950s and attributed that change to better diet (more protein and fresh vegetables) and an increased emphasis on exercise programs.[10]

So what's this got to do with how we use standardized tests? More than might at first meet the eye. Our point is not to support or dispute the data reported in these articles. Instead, we want to call attention to the kind of thinking that readers must do once they confront an apparently simple set of data. This is where *the drawing of inferences about what data mean* comes into play. And it is a process that is inherently complex, like all human thought worthy of the name, and requires that we draw on knowledge and information outside the data at hand.

Note the arresting headline of the British article: "Americans Shrinking as Junk Food Takes Its Toll." Clearly, the writer implies that American consumption of junk food has led to a relative decline in our average height—at least our rate of increase in height has slowed enough to allow other nations to catch up. That could be part of the explanation. But what about the changing demography of the United States? The United States now has a larger number of citizens who are first- or second-generation immigrants from all parts of Asia (remember those short Japanese!) as well as Mexico and Central America. People from both regions tend to be shorter than average white Americans, especially so for the first few generations. Could their presence have an impact? Probably. But even when the data are sliced in such a way that only "white" Americans are measured, the Dutch are still taller.

What else could be at work? Well, Komlos did speculate about the prevalence of junk food in the United States, so the headline writer wasn't making things up, but he also mentioned the lack of health care for many millions of Americans, while their European counterparts generally have lifelong access to quality health care, including prenatal care. Of course, we see which topic caught the fancy of the headline writer.

But whether it's explaining something as supposedly simple as height or as obviously complex as student "achievement," we come back to the messy process of inference—deciding what a set of data means. How completely do our findings represent the area we're interested in? How might they change if we asked different questions? In different ways? At different times?

INFERENCES ABOUT TEACHERS AND SCHOOLS

So far, we've been discussing the use of standardized test scores to make judgments about the "achievement" of individual students. But we promised at the beginning of this chapter that we would say a few things about the use of standardized test scores to evaluate the performance of teachers and even schools or programs. And we like to keep our promises.

Student test scores are used routinely—and with increasing zeal—to make judgments about the performance of teachers and the success of schools and programs. It's convenient and inexpensive because we already have truck-loads of test scores that we can redirect for these purposes. Let's take a look at some of the practical problems with such plans, as well as looking briefly at how well the scores on standardized tests support the inferences we might draw about teachers and schools. (In what follows, most of what we say about the use of test scores to evaluate teacher performance applies equally well to school or program evaluation.)

Suppose you knew of a fourth-grade teacher—let's call him Bob—who looked at the results of his state's reading test and saw that the overall scores for his class showed that more than 80 percent of his students had scored at or above the proficiency level set by the state. On individual skill areas, his class sometimes reached 90 percent proficiency. His school, too, posted proficiency scores some 10 percent higher than the state average. Isn't Bob a great teacher? Maybe we should give him a raise or a bonus. And what about his school's success? Surely we ought to reward the principal and all the rest of the teachers as well.

These are not idle questions in that the Obama administration's "blueprint" makes much of the importance of "effective teachers" and hopes to evaluate and reward them, at least in part, on their *students'* performance. How much of that performance do you think will be measured by anything other than test scores? In March 2010, President Obama piled on in the case of the Central Falls, Rhode Island, teachers and administrators who were fired because the students in their school, located in a low-income district, continued to post low scores.

Once again, if a solution to a problem in education seems too simple and easy, it almost certainly is. What's more, doesn't it raise questions in your mind when the answer to any question about judging performance in education—be it student, teacher, or school performance—is always the same? It's always test scores. The old proverb—if the only tool you have is a hammer, everything will look like a nail—surely applies here. But before we employ our all-purpose educational tool to reward stellar teacher Bob and his school or to bludgeon his less fortunate colleagues across town, let's look at some of the reasons why we might want to think twice.

First, with regard to using their students' test scores to judge teachers' performance, one obvious point isn't often mentioned: you'd have to test a lot more. Why? In discussing this topic, Tom Toch, a longtime education journalist who was also a founder and codirector of the policy analysis think tank Education Sector, pointed out that "only about half of public school teachers teach the subjects or at the grade levels where students are tested."[11] Remember that the tests mandated by No Child Left Behind during its first five years and continued in the Obama administration's "blueprint" occur in grades 3 through 8 and once in high school and that they cover only reading and math. The new Obama administration "blueprint" maintains this testing schedule. What's more, in schools with a departmental structure, such as high schools and many middle schools, only teachers who teach math or English have students who are regularly tested for school accountability. Science was recently added to the testing regimen, and it became an officially tested area in the 2009–2010 school year, so it's a bit early to specify the problems that will emerge. But some of us shudder at the magnitude of the content sampling problem that an area as broad as "science" poses for the test makers, test takers, and test users.

All of this means that judging teachers' performance by student test scores would require us to expand our testing programs so that all high school teachers are included, along with all the teachers who teach at grade levels below third grade, where current accountability testing programs typically begin. And let's not forget the social studies/history teachers in middle schools. Or the teachers of art, music, and physical education at all levels. There goes the budget for assessment! This fact alone probably dooms the adoption of the idea on a broad scale.

Then there's the problem that the tests were created to measure the performance of *populations of individuals*—not that of schools or teachers. Granted, we've just spent a lot of time and effort explaining that they don't do a very good job of measuring that individual performance. How likely is it that, having failed to achieve their intended purpose very well, these tests would all of a sudden prove to be just the thing for judging the impact of teaching on larger groups of students—from individual classes to schools and districts? If you add up all of the problems the tests exhibit for individual students and create a teacher or school score, the original problems won't magically disappear. The tests will still measure only "a narrow band of mostly low-level skills," they'll still consist mostly of questions that about half the students get right, they still won't measure creativity or motivation, and they'll still reward superficial thinking. Only now, the information you derive about the teacher's effectiveness will represent a sort of average student performance based on the scores of a group of students. And knowing that this "average" has risen over the course of the year won't tell you whether a teacher has been as effective with high achievers as with those in the middle or those at the bottom of the test-score heap.

If the number of students in the groups whose scores you're using is large enough—say, a few hundred—you'll at least have some reliability (see "Say What? An Abbreviated Glossary" for a definition); that is, the scores will tend to be similar from one assessment to the next. But when you're talking about rating teachers, all bets are off. An elementary teacher will have only about twenty-five students in her classroom each year, and even an overburdened high school teacher will have only 150 or so students, and not all of them will be taking the same courses. It doesn't take very many super-quick learners to raise that elementary classroom score in a given year or very many challenged learners to bring it back down in the following year. And the teacher wouldn't be responsible for either outcome. While this fact strikes us as obvious, maybe it helps to hear it in the form of an old saw that is well known to many educators: *only attendance is compulsory; learning is optional.*

But what about the need to sort the wheat from the chaff? Don't we want to reward good teachers and either help bad ones improve or get them out of the classroom altogether? Of course, we'd like to do both of these things, but the hammer we happen to have in hand just isn't the tool for the job.

And what do we mean when we say we want to reward good teachers? Most of us would say that a good teacher is successful in helping students learn things we all believe are important. But this definition—though it's one we accept and believe most people would endorse—presents several major problems for judging teacher performance.

The *first* problem has to do with the tests used. If your state uses a traditional standardized achievement test for students, it is probably one of these four: the Iowa Tests of Basic Skills, the California Achievement Tests, the Stanford Achievement Tests, or the Terra Nova tests.[12] These are "norm-referenced" (see the glossary for a definition), and so their main purpose is comparative. They were designed to spread out students' scores along a "bell curve," and that's why the tests consist of items that about half of all students will get right. But shouldn't nearly all students get some things right? If something is critical for third-graders to know, then we should work as hard as we can to see that as many of them as possible learn it, and a fair test of those efforts on our part can't consist of items specifically chosen because half the students get them wrong. And a fair judgment of a teacher's performance can't be based on any test designed in such a way.

Which brings us to the *second* problem for judging teacher performance by means of standardized-test scores. Since all states try to embody in their state-level content standards the things deemed important for students to learn, why can't we just design a "criterion-referenced" test (see the glossary for a definition) that will measure how well students meet those standards for all the subjects and grade levels? The short answer is that there are just too many state content standards to be covered. Recall our discussion in chapter 2 of the problem of covering all fifty-eight subtopics in fourth-grade math. It's easy to see that covering all grades and all subjects would lead to a perfect Catch-22: we have no time left for learning content, because we need to use all available time to assess learning and prepare for more assessments.

James Popham highlights the *third* big problem with using standardized tests to judge teacher performance: "Half or more of what's tested wasn't even supposed to be taught in a particular district or state."[13] Popham refers to this alarming fact as a "teaching/testing mismatch." It stems from a combination of the proliferation of standards and the need to spread scores out, the first two reasons why student scores aren't a good way of judging teachers' performance. If you tell teachers that it's *crucial* for students in fourth grade to learn their multiplication tables up through the tens, as in the Indiana standards we cited before, then don't be surprised if that's what the teachers teach and what the students learn. But don't be surprised if there isn't very much about it on the test. After all, a question that 80 percent or more of the students get right just won't spread the scores enough. Here's Popham's simple syllogism:

> Thus, the more important the content, the more likely teachers are to stress it. The more that teachers stress important content, the better the students will do on an item measuring that content. But the better that students do on such an item, the more likely it is that the item will disappear from the test.[14]

How fair—or sensible—is it to evaluate a teacher's performance by *not measuring* precisely those items that the teacher was told were important, that she consequently stressed throughout her instruction, and that the students learned well as a result? Better to catch everyone out with items that "behave well"—that about 50 percent of students get wrong—but don't necessarily sample the most important parts of the curriculum. If you have the feeling that you're back with Alice on the wrong side of the looking glass, believe us when we say that you are not alone.

Finally, back to Bob, our exemplary fourth-grade teacher. How do we decide just how exemplary Bob's performance and that of his school really is? Toch put the difficulties as well as we could:

> [T]hen there's the daunting challenge of separating out individual teachers' impact on their students' reading and math scores from the myriad other influences on student achievement, and the difficulty of drawing the right conclusions about teacher performance from very small numbers of student test scores, a particular challenge in elementary schools, where teachers work with a single classroom's worth of students most of the day.[15]

Exactly. We mentioned above the problem that small numbers of students pose for judging classroom teachers. But we'd like to know if you've been thinking about some of those other influences that Toch mentions, so here's a test item we've created to see if you've been following our discussion. (If you are a teacher who is not also a parent, simply change the question to refer to your classroom or school.) Consider yourself part of our "norming" sample. We hope the experience doesn't conjure up any unpleasant flashbacks to No. 2 pencils and smudge-filled answer sheets.

Q. If 85 percent or more of the students in your child's classroom or school meet or exceed the proficiency standards set by your state, that means:

   a) your child has an exemplary teacher.
   b) your school has an exemplary principal.
   c) both a and b.
   d) your school community is wealthier than average.
   e) all, any combination, or none of the above.

We trust that all of you answered "e." If not, perhaps another story will drive home the essential unfairness of judging the worth of one person's performance on the basis of other people's actions. This unfairness has nothing to do with the psychometric limitations of standardized tests. Suppose you regularly attend one of the fitness classes at a neighborhood health spa and that weight loss is the primary goal of the classes. To improve its performance, the club wants to identify and reward good fitness teachers and identify and help (or fire) poor ones. Sounds good so far. More fitness for your money is in the offing. Because the goal is weight loss, the club decides to rate teachers according to how much weight (adjusted for starting weights) each instructor's classes lose on average. Teachers of classes that lose more than average will be rewarded; teachers of the less successful classes will have some explaining to do.

Do you feel somewhat uneasy about this system of rating performance? We think you should. Even if a fitness class meets for five hours a week—like an algebra class in your local middle school—there are still 163 hours each week that are outside the teacher's control or direct influence. Yet the fitness teachers will be judged as if they are responsible for any Cinnabons their students consume on the way home from class. Students who indulge their urges for large, syrupy coffees will likewise reflect badly on their teachers' performance reviews. What's more, teachers will be deemed less successful if their students chose the riding mower over the walk-behind or pass up the rake in favor of the leaf blower.

We turn to Koretz for a simple summary of the limitations of test scores for judging *schools*:

> [The] most important reason scores cannot tell you whether a school is good or bad is that schools are not the only influence on test scores. Other factors, such as the educational attainment and educational goals of parents, have a great impact on students' performance. Separating the impact of school quality from the powerful effects of the many out-of-school influences on achievement is a very difficult task, and it can't be done with the data typically available to school systems. The result: one can safely assume neither that schools with the largest score gains are in fact improving the most rapidly nor that those with the highest scores are the best.[16]

Someone needs to tell this to the nation's corps of realtors! The principal of your child's school may be the one in a hundred who is inspiring, capable of helping individual teachers, gifted in how he relates to both children and parents, and an all-American when it comes to running interference between the state and district offices and the classrooms in his school. If so, hang onto him. He's a rare bird indeed. He may be all of these things, but the students' much-higher-than-average test scores still can't be attributed primarily to him. Likewise, the teachers may be, without exception, top flight. Still, those stellar scores can't be explained by their efforts alone either.

Why not? If the school is in a wealthy community, we know that students will post higher test scores. To be sure, the principal and the teachers will have an impact, but what the students bring to school will play a large role as well. Or if a large proportion of the school's parents hold bachelor's or higher degrees, as is the case in many wealthy suburban communities and in some communities clustered around research parks and universities, we know that the students will post high test scores. Again, the school staff will have an influence, but so will the home environments of the students, including good diets and proper health care; the focus on education in highly educated families; the opportunities to learn outside of school and to travel during school vacations; and, yes, the additional financial resources that the school will have at its disposal.

Moreover, these outside-of-school influences tend to flock together like the proverbial birds of a feather. Students whose parents didn't graduate from high school or do not speak English in the home tend not to live in wealthy suburbs or in faculty enclaves near universities. Many of them live at or below the poverty level. The test scores of the schools these children attend also reflect the influence of these extraschool factors, and in this case, they are likely to depress the scores.

We've said before that we don't oppose the judicious use of standardized tests, and we and those whom we asked for comments will have more to say on that score throughout this book. But the inherent unfairness of allowing the scores on standardized tests to be our primary—in some cases, our only—way of judging school quality is one of the cruel ironies of the way public education in America has evolved.

But aren't standardized test scores objective? Don't we need to rely on them for that reason? How do we get objective measures of all those valuable traits like creativity and perseverance that Bracey mentioned? Or of all those outside-of-school influences on schools, teachers, and students also cited in this chapter? The short answer is that you don't and that the standardized test scores won't help much either. The reasons they don't help are the subject of chapter 4.

Testing Autobiography: Phil's Story

I can recall taking *just one* standardized test during my elementary years, an IQ test given in the eighth grade. I know it was an IQ test only because the teacher said it would tell us "how smart we were." But this didn't matter to me and most of my classmates. We knew we were smart enough to work on the farm and hold down the jobs available in our community. And we also knew that we weren't going to college and that the military—the one realistic option for those who wanted to move away from our rural community— didn't seem to care much about IQ either.

Standardized tests then essentially disappeared from my school experience until my senior year in high school. And then it wasn't the SAT or any other college admissions test. Instead, it was the Minnesota MultiPhasic Test for Occupational Aptitude that informed me that I was good with my hands and would be smart to pursue a career where I could use my manual dexterity. I was unimpressed because I planned to join the U.S. Air Force and learn to fly airplanes.

During the summer following my graduation, I was encouraged to attend college by an unusual source. He was a family friend and handyman who did an array of chores around our home. He harped on the importance of education and allowed that he wouldn't have to do all of this "grunt work" if he had a college education.

But I wasn't tuned in. I had already completed the medical examination for the U.S. Air Force and was waiting for my orders to report. But he was persistent and persuasive. Out of the blue came his offer to help me pay for at least the first year of college. How? First, he bought my car, which I couldn't have brought to campus in any case, and then he set me up with a part-time job with a friend of his. In fact, I began working before I began classes. I accepted his offer because college seemed like something that would be both enlightening and enjoyable. What's more, until I found my own place, I could live with an older brother who was then a married senior living off campus. It was far too late for me to even consider a dorm assignment, and dorms were too expensive. When I did find a room in a local rooming house, the weekly rate was $4—not much more than a gallon of gas as I write this!

Paperwork was completed and mailed in, and, as miracles happen, I was accepted and found my way to Bloomington, Indiana, as a freshman at Indiana University. None of this involved test scores of any kind. I submitted a transcript of grades, a recommendation from my high school principal, and the information that I had graduated in the upper half of my class. Of course, there were only sixty in my graduating class.

I graduated from IU in 1961, four years after being admitted. Armed with a license to teach elementary school, I was hired immediately by the local school district and taught there for three years. Then a chance to attend graduate school cropped up. My always supportive wife (now my co-author) said to go for it, so in another one of those last-minute decisions, I became a grad student.

Where was the Graduate Record Examination in all of this? In 1964, I wasn't required to take the GRE before being admitted to the Graduate School of Education at IU. My transcript showed that my grades improved dramatically when, in my sophomore year, I was married. Apparently, that was a good-enough indicator that I would be a serious student. Not only was I admitted to graduate school, but I also received a graduate assistantship. Three years later, I received my EdD in education with a minor in psychology.

The research project I was hired to help administer as a grad assistant was being directed by one of the most highly respected researchers in the nation. It was during this research project that I got my first clue about any problems with standardized testing. We needed to use a standardized test that had several forms, for we had several different groups to test and felt that multiple forms would serve our needs best. I discovered, quite by accident, that on two of the forms the same raw score produced a six-month difference in grade equivalents. At the time, I didn't think of this as a problem with the test; it was just something we had to be aware of when we selected pretests and posttests to administer to specific groups. We needed to be aware that a particular pairing of test forms could produce a six-month gain in the subjects' scores when in fact no improvement had actually happened. It was just one more issue to keep track of when planning the testing program for the treatment and control groups.

I spent fifteen years in this research setting. And over those years, I depended on standardized test scores and accepted them completely. During all that time, I never seriously questioned the results of our research. Everyone knew there was nothing wrong with the tests.

So for the first seventeen years of my professional career, you could call me a supporter of standardized tests, and I defended their use in numerous ways. I never once considered that I would one day come to see them as the most troubling part of our education system.

I first got an inkling of the problems with the uses that schools made of standardized tests when my children began their high school program. We lived in a rural area, and all my children attended the local elementary and middle school. The high school, however, had been consolidated several years earlier. On his first day as a high school freshman, my son came home and showed me his schedule. I was surprised to find that he had been placed in a general math and English class instead of in the algebra and regular English sections.

So, like a good and concerned parent, I phoned to make an appointment to discuss the matter with the counselor. I was further shocked to discover that as a matter of course *all students* from the middle school my children attended were assigned to the lower-level classes. When I pressed a little harder, the counselor admitted that the students had taken a test in eighth grade that was used to determine this placement. While that test score might have satisfied the counselor and the school staff, it didn't satisfy this parent. My son was soon placed where I thought he should be, and he responded well during his high school years. But the experience caused me to begin thinking differently about standardized tests.

My second child always tested well, and because of her competitive nature, always put forth her best effort in testing situations. She moved without a hitch into the regular algebra and English classes and in high school was elected to the National Honor Society.

When my third child reached the beginning of her high school career, she too was denied the algebra class for much the same reason as my son. Once again, I found my way to school, this time to the principal, who offered very little argument before switching her. Eventually, this practice was stopped in our local schools, but I think of the hundreds of students who were misjudged and wrongly placed because a number on a single test had marked them as second rate. My daughter eventually completed a bachelor's degree in quantitative business analysis, with a minor in math.

One final episode involving my family caused me to question the use of standardized tests even more closely. My youngest daughter had no problem with placement in high school. She attended Indiana University and graduated with a degree in kinesiology. She wanted to go to graduate school to study physical therapy but could not gain admittance because of low GRE scores. But she believed in herself and knew that the test scores weren't a true measure of her ability to succeed in graduate school, and, today, she has completed a PhD. (Read our chapter 9, and this story won't surprise you.)

I share this personal experience to show that I have undergone a complete transformation in the way I look at the standardized tests we use in our nation's schools and colleges. I have seen what can happen when the scores are taken as absolute measures of student potential, with little or no consideration given to other kinds of information. My children were lucky enough to have a parent who was able to question such decisions, but not every child is so lucky. And the real tragedy is that no one knows how many children over the years have had their options needlessly limited at such an early point in their school careers. And this experience was far more widespread than just one school system in Southern Indiana.

For myself, I am convinced that, if I had been required to take the various gate-keeping tests now in use, I would be doing something far different today. Thus my current stance: an individual's options should not be limited solely on the basis of scores on any standardized test. No doors should ever be closed on a student's ambitions because of scores on a standardized test. Many other ways exist to make more nuanced judgments: school grades, teacher recommendations, personal interviews, actual performance on similar tasks. These other ways exist; they're just not as cheap.

4

The Tests Are Less Than Objective

Setting standards is a judgment carried out by reasonable people, and it occurs in a social and political context.

—James Pellegrino, University of Illinois at Chicago, 2007

Human beings abhor uncertainty. We're certain about this. If we weren't, we'd have to hate ourselves for being uncertain. And while one of us might well answer to "Dr. Phil," we don't really want to get involved in a long-term therapeutic relationship.

So despite the spread of gambling casinos from state to state, despite the fact that more than forty states operate or at least permit some form of lottery, and despite the stunning growth of online gaming websites, we maintain that people just can't stand uncertainty. How so? People hate living in a state of ambiguity. And when you stop to think about it, there's really no ambiguity in these gambling opportunities. Though we might choose to ignore them, we can know the odds going in. We can know our expected gain (in most cases negative). But we don't have to accept any "fuzzy outcomes." Your six numbers either match the six ping-pong balls sucked up into the tube or they don't.

We want at least as much clarity in the rest of our lives. We want to know that if we take action x, then outcome y will follow. Buy this bond and get a specific dividend in return. Where the learning of our children is concerned, we want "objectivity." We want straightforward reports on their progress that don't depend on the subjective opinions of their teachers and aren't muddied by vague expressions about "potential" or "growth." In short, we want to believe that a test score is a test score is a test score.

So picking up on the questions raised at the end of chapter 3, the assumption about standardized testing that we are exploring in this chapter is: *Standardized tests provide an objective measure of the performance of schools.* We'll treat this assumption as a three-headed one, all three heads having to do with the concept of objectivity. First, there's the assumption that the tests and their creation—the writing and editing of the questions, the setting of passing scores, and so on—really are objective. Second, there's the assumption that the widely reported NAEP levels of achievement, because they are based on test scores, are more objective than other kinds of measures that might be used to report on the performance of our children and educational institutions. Finally, we ask why we have so placidly accepted the verdict of the test scores. In other words, though the numerical data seem to tell their own story, why have we accepted it as always the "true" story?

While we may want to remove the human element, which can be unreliable, from the process of judging our children's achievement, that's not the way things work with our schools and the children and adults who inhabit them. And it never can be. We'll show that the human element is always present in the daily work of schools, and it is likewise always present, one way or another, in the ways we assess them.

THE TESTS THEMSELVES

But first let's be clear about the term *objectivity* itself. In his years as an editor, Bruce deleted nearly all of those opening paragraphs beginning "Webster's defines" such and such a word as. . . . In this case, however, we want to be sure you understand which of the many senses of "objective" is typically used when referring to standardized tests. Remembering all those direct quotes that ended up on the office floor, we'll paraphrase rather than quote our dictionary. By "objective," we mean based on observable phenomena and not influenced by emotion or personal prejudice.

This definition certainly fits with the kind of commentary you might have seen in your local newspapers. For instance, any time complaints about college admissions tests are voiced and someone suggests replacing them with high school grades, the response is likely to make the following points: We need to be able to tell whether an A at one school means the same thing as an A at another school. To do that we need a common yardstick. Standardized tests are our best yardsticks because they yield an "objective" measure of a student's or a school's performance. Case closed.

Now that you've read the preceding chapters, we think you can see some of the holes in this argument. For example, we showed in chapter 3 that "test scores" are not the same as "achievement" and in chapter 2 that the scores represent a sampling of just a small slice of a particular kind of performance in a particular part of a domain of knowledge. These counterarguments should be sufficient to pour cold water on the most heated of the boosters of objective tests. In what follows, we'll seek to put to rest claims about the "objectivity" of standardized tests by looking, first, at how they're made and then at what the precision of their scores does—and doesn't—mean.

So where do these tests come from? Someone, somewhere has to create them. Who are these people, what are they trying to accomplish, and where do they get their questions? Well, one way they get questions for at least some tests is by advertising for freelancers to submit them—for the princely sum of two dollars for each accepted question. What a scientific process! If you'd like to supplement your income in these difficult times, here's a link to just such an offer: http://www.ifreelance.com/project/detail. aspx?projectid=28067. The site is fishing for questions from freelancers to use for the College-Level Examination Program (CLEP) mathematics test. This is the test that many colleges use to award credit to students for things they've learned outside the formal school or college classroom. The guidelines for submitted questions are:

Each question must contain the following:

   a. the question itself
   b. five potential answers
   c. highly detailed, step-by-step explanation that shows how to get the correct answer

Not much to go on there. But any questions that meet the guidelines will be submitted to a test development committee at the College Board.[1] This committee consists of three or four faculty members who teach in the content area covered by the exam. That seems reassuring. These subject specialists, for that's what they are, "review and shape" the questions regularly. Other item development committees use feedback from national surveys to "establish test specifications that determine the content of exams" and "establish a set of skills and knowledge requirements that successful test takers should be able to demonstrate." They have other responsibilities as well, including guiding new questions from their "raw" form through editing and review and pretesting. Curiously, the CLEP website says that items may originate "either with members of the test development committee or with other faculty members in the discipline who have been commissioned to write items." We're not sure where that leaves the "freelancers" who are invited to submit questions, but it's clear that a great deal of responsibility falls on the members of the item development committee to sort out good questions from bad or to rewrite them altogether. The content specialists are assisted by assessment specialists. Most of the other activities of this committee are related to policy and promotion.

Then there are committees of fifteen to twenty college faculty members who periodically convene—these days, mostly online—to review standards and make recommendations for what constitutes a passing score. Currently, that figure is a scaled score of 50, where scores range from 20 to 80. (See "Say What? An Abbreviated Glossary" for a definition of a scaled score, but simply add zero to the scores here, and you have the familiar 200-800 scale of the SAT, itself a scaled score.) The process of setting the standards and choosing which questions represent which levels of difficulty is complex and time-consuming and includes matching an estimate of the kind of student who would answer a given question correctly to a profile of a typical A, B, C, or D student of the tested subject.

We've offered this much detail—and there's lots more that we are sparing you—on the CLEP test because the College Board puts a great many resources into the effort to make the test a good measure of what students would learn in a given college-level course. And because the domain of this test is restricted to the learning covered in a single course, it is a somewhat less daunting task than measuring a student's "achievement" in an area as broad as, say, all of precollege mathematics. But one thing that this complex process demonstrates clearly is that it involves considerable judgment on the part of many individuals. From the freelancer who submits a question to the committees that review it to the assessment specialists who decide whether a question is well behaved, there is considerable subjectivity. It's simply unavoidable. The College Board does what it can to reduce that subjectivity, but a good deal remains nonetheless.

Furthermore, there is additional subjectivity in the setting of the passing score, and it is also unavoidable. The CLEP test uses what is known as the modified Angoff method of setting a passing score. This means that the panel of content experts examines a question and decides, in CLEP's case, what percentage of A students (or B students, or C students, etc.) would be able to answer correctly. The scores proposed by the panel members are then averaged to arrive at a passing score. The process is an attempt to reach something like consensus, but certainly a great deal of subjectivity is included in any kind of "estimate" of how many students at each level could answer a question correctly.

We aren't arguing that the subjectivity of the CLEP test renders it bad or that the test doesn't serve a purpose. Over the years, many individuals have benefited from the college credit they obtained as a result of this test. But there's nothing objective about the way the test is created, and human judgment and experience play a role at every step in its creation. So put up your skepticism antennae when you read the next newspaper report on the release of a new batch of "objective" data.

THOSE NAEP ACHIEVEMENT LEVELS

Many of the arguments swirling around testing these days have to do with the relationship of the test scores to standards or proficiency levels, and the standards and proficiency levels that are judged most critical in U.S. education these days are the proficiency levels of the National Assessment of Educational Progress (NAEP). But these are no more natural features of the universe than the items used on the CLEP test. So we pose the same question about the standards and proficiency levels that we asked about the test items: Where do they come from anyway? Your local newspaper reports your state's test scores and even lists each of your local schools along with its percentage of students in each tested grade who reach the "proficient" or the "advanced" or the "basic" level. What are they talking about? Where do these levels come from? The news media scarcely ever explore what proficiency means.

A decade ago, when students' performance as judged by these NAEP proficiency levels was being used primarily to argue for a national achievement test, Richard Rothstein pointed out for his readers the inadequacy of the process of setting the NAEP levels. His words are just as apt today, when the notion of national standards and a national test has acquired renewed vigor:

> The procedure for defining these achievement levels, in reality, is both ideologically and technically suspect. The standards seem to have been established primarily for the purpose of confirming preconceptions about the poor performance of American schools. The specification of such levels is an extraordinarily complex undertaking; it would challenge even the most expert psychometricians.[2]

More recently, Rothstein joined forces with two education researchers, Rebecca Jacobsen and Tamara Wilder, in a book titled *Grading Education*. Chapter 4 of their book takes on the NAEP proficiency levels directly and even quotes a publication by the National Assessment Governing Board, the group that sets the widely publicized proficiency levels. Here is the passage Rothstein and his colleagues quote:

> Nor is performance at the Proficient level synonymous with "proficiency" in the subject. That is, students who may be considered proficient in a subject, given the common usage of the term, might not satisfy the requirements for performance at the [Proficient] NAEP achievement level.[3]

It probably won't surprise you to learn that "the most expert psychometricians" are not exactly the ones who decide where the levels are set. The levels and the cut scores used to determine whether or not students are proficient are set by the National Assessment Governing Board, a body that consists of a sampling of politicians, policy makers, educators, and others. Try not to hum "The Twelve Days of Christmas" while you read the following list of NAGB's members:

> Two Governors, or former Governors, of different political parties
> Two state legislators of different political parties
> Two chief state school officers
> One superintendent of a local education agency
> One member of a state board of education
> One member of a local board of education
> Three classroom teachers representing the grade levels (4th, 8th, and 12th) at which the National Assessment is conducted
> One representative of business or industry
> Two curriculum specialists
> Three testing and measurement experts
> One nonpublic school administrator or policymaker
> Two school principals, one elementary and one secondary
> Four additional members who are representative of the general public, including parents
> The Director of the Institute of Education Sciences (ex-officio)

And a partridge in a . . . Sorry. The views of all these folks should surely be represented in determining "what students should know and be able to do." This phrase has become the current short version of what standards in education are supposed to spell out. But measurement expert James Pellegrino reminds us that "setting standards is a judgment carried out by reasonable people, and it occurs in a social and political context."[4] As the researcher Richard Shavelson put it at the 1997 CRESST Conference, where the main topic was the search for ways to make any national test a valid one:

> Judgment plays a role in everything we do. Setting standards is extraordinarily complex and . . . we have not come to grips with the judgment process around indicators of what is good enough.[5]

In other words, the NAEP achievement levels are, first and foremost, policy statements, not scales in any way comparable to measures of height or weight. And how the achievement levels are set has proved troublesome. Education researcher Gerald Bracey summed up the serious concerns about the NAEP achievement levels this way:

The NAEP achievement levels—basic, proficient, and advanced—have been rejected by everyone who has studied them: the General Accounting Office, the National Academy of Education, the National Academy of Sciences, and the Center for Research in Evaluation, Student Standards and Testing (CRESST, co-headquartered at UCLA and the University of Colorado, Boulder), as well as by individual psychometricians such as Lyle V. Jones of the University of North Carolina.[6]

Questions that relate to the NAEP achievement levels have been raised about the appropriateness of setting cut scores between, say, the proficient and basic levels. How many more questions must a student answer correctly to be deemed proficient? These are serious technical questions that the psychometricians on the panel and on the outside evaluating teams have raised and continue to debate. But, because they are both complex and technical, none of them have penetrated the consciousness of the policy makers who wring their hands about our failing schools and poorly educated students or the journalists who take part in the national feeding frenzy that occurs with every release of a new set of test scores—whether NAEP scores or scores that have been equated to the NAEP.

Even The Daily Howler—a Washington, D.C., media watchdog website—has chimed in. The Howler focused on a debate in the *Washington Post* between Ross Wiener of the Education Trust and Gerald Bracey (www.dailyhowler.com/dh01#13B9A0). The Howler picked up a quote Bracey used from the study by the National Academy of Sciences: "NAEP's current achievement level-setting procedures remain fundamentally flawed, appropriate validity evidence for the cut scores is lacking, and the process has produced unreasonable results." Bracey then asked:

What does the National Academy of Sciences consider an "unreasonable result"? Just this: In the Third International Mathematics and Science Study, American fourth-graders ranked third in science among the 26 participating nations. Yet only 30 percent scored proficient on the NAEP's science assessment. Only 30 percent of our world-beating kids are proficient? Unreasonable. Ludicrous.

But The Howler expands on Bracey's point and inadvertently helps us make ours:

When we set the standard for "passing" a test of this type, it *always involves subjective judgments.* [Emphasis added.] What sorts of things must fifth-graders do to be judged "proficient" in reading (or math)? We can try to tie our answer to traditional notions of "grade level" work. But those traditional notions of "grade level" work weren't taken from tablets which Moses delivered.

Presumably, conventional notions of "fifth-grade work" are based on observations of past fifth-grade kids. But there has never been a time when fifth-graders all functioned at the same level. To what level should a fifth-grader be held? Inevitably, that's a matter of judgment. And oh yes! Wherever you end up setting the bar, it will be far below where some kids are working—and far above the functioning level of other fifth-grade kids.

Remember, kids are different! Consider reading, for example. In America today, many fifth-graders can handle books written on traditional sixth- or seventh-grade level (or beyond). And many fifth-graders are functioning years below grade level—or are barely able to read at all. What must fifth-graders do before we say that they are "proficient"? Inevitably, that's a subjective judgment. We can set the bar as high (or as low) as we want. In the end, there's no "right" answer.

No right answer. We couldn't have said it better ourselves, and it brings us to the question: Just how clear a story do these numbers tell?

Again, the first thing to get out of the way is what we mean by "objective" in this context. Beginning with our earlier definition of *objective*—based on observable phenomena and not influenced by emotion or personal prejudice—what can we say about standardized test scores? We've shown above that there is always subjectivity in the selection of items and the setting of standards. So what's left that might account for the claim that standardized tests are objective? The only part of standardized testing that truly deserves to be called objective is the scoring. This means that the same black mark on one kid's answer sheet will be scored in the same way as a similar mark on a classmate's.

When you say it that way, it doesn't seem to add up to much, does it? It's certainly not the firmest of foundations on which to build a national education policy. But when commentators toss around a word so freighted with positive connotations, readers and listeners can easily be led to believe that such a completely "objective yardstick" actually exists. But that yardstick is made up of the scores on standardized tests, which, it is argued, can then be used to rank schools, teachers, and students in an unambiguous way. We beg to differ.

First, there's not much that's unambiguous about any standardized test score. All tests have measurement error (see the glossary for a definition), perhaps only plus or minus a couple of percentage points on well-designed, nationally marketed tests. But a couple of percentage points either way can mean that one student doesn't graduate while another does, when we can't say with confidence that their test scores really differ. If the margin of error on a test is ±3 percent, and your score is 1 percent above the cut score for graduation, while my score is 1 percent below, does that mean your "true score" for the test is 2 percent higher than mine? No, we can't say that, at least not with the 95 percent confidence that we'd like to have. What we can say with full confidence is that our scores are indistinguishable. If we took the test tomorrow, our positions could easily reverse, and no one should be surprised.

If you think that treating test scores in this way means that you can't simply do with them anything that you'd like to do, then you have been paying attention. You can't treat an individual's test score as a clean, crisp number. Remember what they told us in high school chemistry? You can't know the location and momentum of an electron at the same time, so the books illustrated this curious phenomenon with drawings of fuzzy and oddly shaped "orbitals" that showed a probability distribution where the electron was likely to be. Remembering these drawings can be a helpful way to think about test scores. Think of them as fuzzy little ranges that extend both above and below the score and show where the "true score" is *likely* to be—though 5 percent of the time it will be outside that range.

You would think that those who cover education—and so spend at least some time reporting on test scores—would be clear about this and would want to make sure to remind the public. But, with rare exceptions, you would be wrong.

Here's the lead from the story in our local newspaper reporting the release of the fall 2008 ISTEP+ test scores here in Indiana: "This year's state test scores show Monroe County Community School Corp. exceeding state averages and its own 2007 pass rates."[7] Good news, yes? The superintendent deserves a raise? Well, not so fast. The percent passing (that is, reaching the state's cut score) for our district moved up in 2008 all right. In English/language arts it moved from 76 percent passing in 2007 to 77 percent in 2008. In math, the change was from 77.8 percent to 79.2 percent. Yippee! Where are our party hats?

But before we celebrate too long and loud, remember those fuzzy ranges and remember, too, that one big thing changed during the intervening year: the students are not the same. So even if these scores differed by enough to allow us to say that the district's true performance was likely to be better— and they don't—we'd have to qualify that claim by considering the changed student population: today's tenth-graders, for example, weren't tested last year when they were ninth-graders.

But there's more to the false precision that the numerical scores on standardized tests encourage than just overlooking the fuzziness of the scores. The use of averages, which is clearly handy, *always obscures at least as much information as it reveals.* We mentioned in chapter 3 that an average doesn't tell you anything about the performance of the highest or lowest achievers. And this problem doesn't go away when you gather up the scores from all the schools in a state and average them.

Consider again the 2008 ISTEP+ testing for our district. What does the 77 percent pass rate in English/language arts mean for the schools and grades that parents care most about, the ones their kids attend? In 2008, the percent passing both the math and English/language arts tests for each of the grades tested (3, 4, 5, 6, 7, 8, and 10) ranged from 68 percent to 76 percent. (For passing math only, the range was from 72 percent to 86 percent; for English only, from 75 percent to 80 percent.) Now a difference of eight percentage points is more likely to be real than the one-point difference overall, but hold on. Even if your child is in the 76 percent grade, that figure is an average of data from the fourteen elementary schools in the district (or the three middle schools or two high schools). And when you get to the school-level scores, you will have more than one class to average. When you get to the classroom level, you will have about twenty-five individuals to average. And the fuzziness of these average test scores grows ever fuzzier as the numbers get smaller.

Now, we don't object to reporting averages. They are handy mathematical tools for debating complicated issues. What we object to is phony interpretation, and even our former state superintendent has been guilty. Again from our local newspaper, but clearly verified in the state department's own press releases, we have this:

> Superintendent of Public Instruction Suellen Reed said in a news release that statewide, the results are disappointing. English pass rates dropped by one percentage point at every grade level except 10th grade, which remained the same as in 2007. Pass rates for math and science were mixed, with changes ranging from a two-point gain to a two-point decline.[8]

What reporters and bureaucrats need to say to people is that the state scores have remained stable since at least 2004. Why? Because English/language arts scores yielded 71.2 percent passing in 2004 and never went higher than 72 percent or lower than 71 percent over the five-year period. Math pass rates were 72.2 percent in 2004 and never went higher than 74.6 percent over the same five years. So our fuzzy little spheres of test scores are bobbing along nicely, hovering steadily just about where they were five years ago.

What explains the nearly obsessive drive to report these numbers and track the minuscule changes in them as if they had earth-shaking importance? It's certainly true that Americans—indeed, nearly everyone in the developed world—looks on numbers with a combination of fascination and fear.

Look at the college ratings, an annual insanity begun in earnest by *U.S. News & World Report* but copied by a number of other publications. (For a new perspective on these rankings, check out the college rankings done by the *Washington Monthly*; they turn some of the *U.S. News* ratings upside down merely by using a slightly different set of criteria.) Most university administrators will acknowledge privately—or anonymously on the website of the *Chronicle of Higher Education*—that they believe the rankings are less than helpful to prospective students and their parents. But these administrators simply can't fight a presentation of such "objective" numerical data—even if the data give, at best, an incomplete, and potentially distorted, picture of their institutions. While many believe that the rankings make it harder for students to find the right college for their needs, they argue that they can't simply stop participating for fear that *U.S. News* will publish information acquired from other, presumably less reliable, sources than the universities themselves.

And public demand for such rankings continues to grow, fueled by credulous reporting in the popular press. On August 24, 2008, under the headline "IU Heading in Right Direction," our local newspaper editorialized that Indiana University "rose from 33rd in 2007 to 30th in 2008 among top public universities, and 75th to 71st in top public and private institutions." Then the editors listed the schools in the Big Ten that had moved up or down one or two slots in the rankings. The conclusion: "What exactly that means is open to interpretation. But it's certainly better to move up than to move down." Maybe, but if those who know the most about our universities don't believe these rankings are valid indicators in the first place, then even that seemingly obvious conclusion might not be warranted.

THE ILLUSORY POWER OF NUMBERS

The illusion of objectivity trumps the considered experience of the presidents and deans of the nation's leading universities. Little more needs to be said about the magical power of numbers. But we feel compelled to ask why the profession of education—from top to bottom—seems to have handed over control to anyone with a dataset, whether the school readiness test scores of preschoolers, the state achievement test scores of ninth-graders, or the SAT scores of incoming college freshmen. Why do we seek reassurance in numbers no matter how sound or unsound, rather than in the judgment of those in the education profession?

There is a large literature on the professions, and a smaller part of it is devoted to the question of when and how professions resort to the apparent objectivity of numbers. The seminal text in this area is a book by Theodore Porter.[9] In a document prepared for a 2006 symposium on evidence-based medicine, Nikolas Rose of the London School of Economics summarized the conditions Porter outlined that encourage a profession to give precedence to numerical data.[10] As you read the items we've taken from Rose's list, keep in mind that he is talking about medicine, among the more robust professions in terms of the autonomy of practitioners and the deference given to professional judgment. How much stronger his points seem when we import them to a field like education, where everything from the education of teachers to the content of the curriculum is continually subjected to hot debate by those outside the profession. Here is a sample of Rose's points:

- Professions turn to numbers not when they are strong, but when they are weak.
- Strong professions have moral authority—even with regard to how their numbers are used and interpreted.
- Professions under criticism need the protection of numbers.

Following up on that last bullet, Rose explained that numbers confer a sense of fairness and impartiality and provide a justification for decisions. Such powers have a strong appeal, especially for professionals and policy makers who are under attack. The numbers, Rose explains, appear to "provide the assurance of objectivity." Remember, too, that these numbers come from various medical tests, which, he points out, were themselves calibrated on specific populations, for specific periods of time, and whose success is judged according to—here we go again—subjective criteria.

Thus even the profession many people would call the most data-driven of all wrestles with precisely the same questions we have been wrestling with in this chapter. Our ability to quantify is a powerful tool, for both the natural and social sciences. But having numbers at our fingertips does not absolve us of the responsibility of making deliberative decisions, engaging in reflection and argument, and, above all, interpreting the numbers we generate. And that interpretation extends far beyond the tools of inferential statistics and includes everything from examining how the devices (whether tests or telescopes) that created the numbers work, how the numbers were generated, and how they will be used.

No one is calling for the elimination of medical tests; rather, the debate is over what the outcomes of the medical tests mean and how they are to be used. And we aren't calling for the total elimination of standardized testing in our schools. However, we do believe that the tests are currently used far too much and that the interpretations of their scores are challenged far less often than they should be.

What we call for is common sense in interpreting what the tests tell us, coupled with a measure of respect for the wisdom of those in the profession. Such an emphasis in school policy making will surely complicate public decisions, but we believe that the resulting decisions will be better for our children and for the nation's future. We believe great harm is done by treating test results, which are gross and fuzzy indicators at best, as if their validity is absolute, their apparent precision is real, and their unexamined outcomes unchallengeable.

In chapter 5, we'll examine a question that's not intrinsic to the tests themselves but involves their widespread use as motivators. Whether we use them for giving rewards or meting out punishments, we rarely ask whether or not they work. In chapter 5, we'll ask.

Testing Autobiography: Bruce's Story

$\mathbf{M}$y earliest memories of tests and testing are uniformly positive. Americans have always loved to rank things, especially ourselves. Back in the 1950s, many newspapers ran Sunday features on IQ tests, and some of those stories included sample tests—with a scoring key and explanatory information. These became even more common for a time shortly after *Sputnik*, when the nation suddenly began to worry that its reservoir of intelligence was running dry. Of course, these tests were very short, and though they were timed, there were no controls whatsoever on how we administered them to ourselves. They should have been published with a prominent "use at your own risk" disclaimer.

But they were just newspaper features, what harm could they do? By themselves, probably not much. But they set the stage for me to accept the outcomes of all sorts of standardized tests, which in those days were almost exclusively timed, multiple-choice tests. My dad and I would take these sample tests whenever they appeared. Then—being both Americans and sports fans—we would compare our scores.

To say that we didn't understand the limitations of the tests would be wrong. We didn't know they *had any* limitations. If you took a test and used the answer key to determine your score, then that score was a scientifically valid number that said something precise about you. Both my dad and I scored well above average, so that meant the tests had to be sound!

But the baby boom had already cut its milk teeth and was arriving at the schoolhouse doors in vast numbers. And those numbers meant the nation needed some mechanism for sorting the winners from the losers in the race to fill the limited places in our universities. Couple that need with the pressure of competing with the Soviet Union and you have ideal conditions for creating a tracked education system that would use "scientific means"—i.e., test scores—to do the tracking.

My school experience of tests began innocently enough with extremely low-stakes achievement tests given in late spring in each year of elementary school. The extent of our "preparation" was a reminder to get a good night's sleep and eat a good breakfast. We got a five-minute "lesson" on the mechanics of the tests just before we were allowed to open our test booklets.

We didn't worry much about the tests or our scores. In fact, I never even learned my scores on any of these tests, and I don't believe my parents did either. Maybe somewhere administrators were feeling agitated if there was a slight downturn in some area, but the tests really did seem to be just one more bit of data to toss into the hopper each year to get an idea of how the school system was doing. To put it in terms appropriate for more recent discussions of testing, these assessments had extremely low stakes.

But competition was in the air. There was a drumbeat, faint at first, but growing ever stronger, that reminded everyone that the baby boom generation was going to have to claw its way into college—and only the best would get there. Facing the prospect of high school, I knew I had better make sure it was a "good high school"—i.e., one that would help me get into college. Since no one in my family had ever even attended college, much less graduated, we were innocent of how colleges select their students. We knew nothing about "legacy" admissions, we believed that student athletes were just students who happened to be good at sports, and we thought that good test scores were absolutely required to get into any college.

But first there was high school. I lived a block outside the city limits and so couldn't attend for free the Baltimore Polytechnic Institute, a top-notch public school with special citywide program for students talented in math and science. Even if I passed the entrance exam, my family would have to pay tuition for me to attend, and that wasn't an option for us. But Baltimore's Catholic "order schools" also featured strong academic programs, and they offered scholarships to those who scored high on the entrance exams.

These entrance exams were much like the end-of-year achievement tests in that they covered a wide range of material. But they were harder and a lot scarier, in part because they were given on the campuses of the schools we hoped to attend, and the proctors were neither nuns nor lay teachers but priests or brothers—men decked out in long cassocks or soutanes with odd variations on the familiar Roman collar.

Roughly half of the students who sat for the exams—a self-selected group to begin with—were accepted, and each school gave four to six scholarships. Once again, testing was good to me. I was again among the top scorers. These tests just had to be right!

Just a couple of years later, all of us faced the PSAT-NMSQT—an unpronounceable acronym for what was then known as the Preliminary Scholastic Aptitude Test and National Merit Scholarship Qualifying Test. Again, the tests told me I was good at this school thing or whatever it was that the tests were measuring. My scores qualified me as a semifinalist and later a finalist. Why would I question a technology that was helping me on my way? Things were working out quite well.

Fast forward another year or so to the SAT, still as scary a prospect for today's students as it was for me back in the fall of 1966. But some things were different. There weren't any review courses. We all believed that you couldn't prepare. That's what the folks at the Educational Testing Service told us, and who were we to contradict the experts? ETS provided a slim pamphlet on flimsy paper that explained the format of the questions and even offered a couple of examples. We all tried them. But for me, at least, that was the extent of my preparation.

But again, my scores were good, and I found myself far out on the right (in both senses) tail of the normal distribution, where the curve gets very close to the baseline and just a few high scorers are clustered. A better place to be than the other end, to be sure, but it may have had less to do with my gaining admission to a top-flight university (I ultimately attended MIT) than I believed at the time. As I was to learn later, a great deal more is involved in selecting a freshman class than merely arranging the applicants in the order of their test scores.

Then just four years or so later, in the late spring of 1971, I found myself talking with a faculty mentor who asked what I intended to do after graduating. To my shrug, he offered the suggestion that, because I was pretty good at writing and literary criticism, I might think about graduate school in an English department. He made a phone call, I made a few more, and soon my materials were on the way to the University of New Hampshire, where I was admitted— late and provisionally, because I had missed every deadline anyone could find. There were no tests required, not that I would have minded, for I still believed that the tests, those impartial judges, would stand by me. They always had.

During the next couple of years, as I finished up a master's degree and began applying to doctoral programs, my faith in testing began to weaken. Once I had finished my degree, I worked full time in the university library where I had access to all the books and periodicals that arrived each day. I saw the newest studies that ranked graduate schools, and I saw the books and articles that raised questions about the sorting and selection of students based on their standardized test scores. The focus of this antitesting literature was primarily college admissions tests because the stakes for testing in most of K–12 education in the early 1970s were just too low to cause much concern. Only the federal Title I program for disadvantaged children had anything like tests with weighty consequences, and those didn't concern the children.

When at last it was time to return to graduate school, my scores on the Graduate Record Examination (GRE) were, if anything, better than those on the SAT. But as far as I know, no one in the department where I earned my doctorate ever even looked at them.

Since those days in the 1970s, I've raised questions about each and every new mandate for testing. Often, just a few common sense questions—nothing technical—are all that's needed to show that tests are simply being used as an administrative convenience. The tests offer administrators and politicians a set of numbers to justify whatever "policy du jour" they are pursuing. Want to get rid of affirmative action in higher education? Let's see what the test scores say. Want to introduce some version of pay for performance and need a scale that seems unambiguous to use for making decisions about teachers' salaries? Here's a boxful of student test scores!

One look at my own nuclear family shows just how pernicious the impact of this worship of the test score has become. I have a wife and two grown daughters. My wife got violently sick before she took the SAT, and there seemed to be no physical cause. What's more, it's not something she has outgrown. While our daughters were in school, she worked the luncheon shift at a local restaurant. When her maturity, work ethic, and organizational skill (she was a mom, remember) led the company to ask her to take their management training, she took the workshops and studied the material. I know she knew it, because I quizzed her on it. When she sat for the test, she froze, as always. She kept her lunch down this time, but the company said it couldn't do anything for her. The test scores, after all, were objective.

Then there are my daughters. Both are now on good paths, working and studying hard in areas they chose and are passionate about. But during the dark night of the high school testing season, the younger one was a dedicated, hard-working student who earned good grades but tested poorly. She decided not even to sit for the AP exam in Calculus 2, though she'd never had a grade lower than an A, and I know she knew the material because I had tutored her. "Why bother?" she said. "I'll just blow it, and I don't mind taking the class again in college. I *like* math."

And her sister? More given to playing around and partying, she had pulled off many a narrow escape, gradewise, because she is a gifted test taker. What's more, though she was an abysmal math student in high school and barely passed the minimum required classes, imagine her friends' surprise when she posted scores one hundred points or more higher than theirs on the SAT. When I asked how she did it, she explained that it was strategy. When she read about how the test was scored, she decided to work to get *all* the easy questions (mostly arithmetic and simple algebra) right, to guess at the tougher ones where she could understand and eliminate more than one answer, and to just pass over the ones that struck her as written in a foreign language. I'm sure her strategy raised her score, but it gave any college admissions officer an erroneous impression of her math skill. You really can game this system, and I swear I didn't tell her how.

So I've come a long way from those days when my dad and I assumed that someone, somewhere had worked out all the details about the validity of the IQ tests we took. I no longer believe that my test scores usefully predicted my performance in high school, in college, or in graduate school. Indeed, my undergraduate performance wouldn't correlate very well with my test scores. Why? See the reference above to my elder daughter's performance. Sex, drugs, and rock 'n' roll will take their toll on anyone's grade-point average!

5

Rewards and Punishments Don't Motivate

> Rewards and punishments can never succeed in producing more than temporary compliance.
>
> —Alfie Kohn, author of *Punished by Rewards*, 1999

There is an old joke that stands clearest in our minds as the caption of a cartoon depicting a group of pirates, some bearing marks of the lash, gathered around a message nailed to the mast and signed from "The Management," that is, the captain. That message reads: The beatings will continue . . . until morale improves. Today, the gag line is common on a T-shirt, paired with a skull and crossbones. Everyone who saw that old cartoon or now reads the T-shirt chuckles. It doesn't matter how often you've heard the joke, because everyone has been someone's crew member—subject to a coercive regimen designed "for their own good." The main characteristic shared by those systems of control we've all been subject to is that they rely on rewards and punishments. And one thing we do know for sure is that such control systems don't work very well, at least not in the long term.

In this chapter, we're moving outward from an examination of the features of standardized tests that was our focus in the preceding chapters and considering one of the primary uses made of the scores. The whole testing apparatus that we've been writing about—from item development to the reporting of results to any follow-up actions taken—is embedded in a system of accountability that has become skewed by its excessive reliance on rewards and punishments. The tests and the scores they generate are seen as levers to be used to move the education system along. Policy makers try to use those levers to move educators and students—never themselves, of course—to take action, and they aren't satisfied that merely reporting the scores along with any other information that the public might need to evaluate its schools (see chapter 1) will be enough to make that happen. So they bring out the big, if ineffective, guns: threats of punishments and promises of rewards.

The underlying assumption about standardized testing that we're looking at in this chapter has to do with the so-called accountability system built on the standardized tests. And this assumption is applied to educators in their workplaces almost as often as it is to students. It goes like this: *Rewards and punishments based on test scores can be used to motivate students and educators.* If you want *students* to focus on their academic work, offer to give them something they like (say, recognition, special privileges, or a pizza party) or threaten to withhold something they desire (say, a weekend free from homework, promotion to the next grade, or high school graduation). If you want *teachers* to do their best to improve their students' learning, offer them something that they want (like higher pay) or threaten to take away something they value (like their autonomy in the classroom or their community's control of its schools). But like the ones before it, this assumption, too, is false.

A WORD ON WORDS

You probably haven't come across the word *punishment* used in the press to refer to anything a school district, state, or the federal government might do to a student or school as part of an effort to improve achievement. And you probably won't see it used when referring to teachers either. We don't "punish" schools for not giving us the test score gains policy makers seek, but we do "sanction" them or, according to the Obama administration's "blueprint," we subject them to "interventions." These latter words sound less personal and less painful than punishments, but there are apt to be just as many tears. Individual kids we can punish, for misbehavior if not for low test scores; schools, we sanction or target for intervention. Moreover, we don't usually talk about "rewards" for schools or for teachers. Again, that seems to be a word that's too personal for use with adults or institutions. While we are sometimes allowed to "reward" kids, what we dangle in front of teachers or schools to motivate them is almost always called an "incentive."

But while the range of connotations between "bribes" on the one hand and "incentives" on the other is broad, there is little difference in their impact. Nor does a "disincentive" feel altogether different from a "punishment." We'll stick with rewards and punishments (or carrots and sticks) in this chapter, but be aware of the sometimes subtle impact of such small changes in wording.

IT'S MOSTLY PUNISHMENT

The best discussion of how punishments and rewards have typically been used in our society is still Alfie Kohn's *Punished by Rewards*.[1] Now more than a decade old, this volume remains worth reading for its cogent argument, supported by voluminous research, that rewards and punishments usually do more harm than good. Kohn has written persuasively elsewhere about standardized tests themselves,[2] but in *Punished by Rewards*, he targets what he calls "pop behaviorism," which is the philosophy derived from behaviorist psychology that accounts for most of the ways we as a society try to "manage" one another. Kohn translates the underlying mechanism into a very simple quid pro quo: "Do this, and you'll get that."

Look around, and you'll see that most of what's done to us by someone else involves this very manipulative trade-off. From child rearing in the home to motivation in the schools to management in the corporate world, it's case after case of "Do this, and you'll get that." It's behaviorism all the way. The psychological theory (and philosophy) of "behaviorism" is a way of looking at animal and human learning that focuses only on objectively observable behaviors and discounts mental activities. To the behaviorist, it doesn't matter what we think we're doing or what we think we mean, because the only things we can observe are behaviors. There is no place for the mind or for intention. When you intend to do something, that intention is just another mental "behavior."

Behaviorism began in the early twentieth century and grew along with the movement toward industrial efficiency, which reached its own zenith in time-and-motion studies. If you remember *Cheaper by the Dozen*—the book or either of the movies—that kind of rationalizing of motion and breaking each task into component parts closely parallels what behaviorism does with the workings of the human brain. For those of us who think about schools, that means learning. Just as a worker's actions are broken into the simplest steps in order to maximize output, so a student's learning is broken into observable (i.e., measurable) parts, which are in turn manipulated through punishments and rewards.

If you've been a casual observer of developments in psychology, watching from the sidelines, you might have thought that behaviorism had pretty much run its course. As the cognitive revolution, which began in the 1950s, sought to establish meaning as the central concept of psychology, behaviorism diminished in importance. But for all its setbacks within the field of psychology, behaviorism has not yielded a yard of territory in the culture at large. And over the past couple of decades or so, it has expanded its influence in the field of education. Beginning with a spate of state-level standardized tests that grew out of the standards movement of the early 1990s, the behaviorist stance of promising rewards and threatening punishments has become standard operating procedure. This test-driven thinking, which gave us the accountability model used by the federal No Child Left Behind law and is still promoted in the new administration's "blueprint," has behaviorism at its core: Set the bar high for test scores, raise it every year, and punish those schools that fail to make it over. The only problem is that, as a motivational tactic, it is ineffective.

We think most Americans would readily agree that using punishment to motivate people to undertake some beneficial action probably isn't a good choice of strategy. While there are still advocates for stern approaches to discipline, we've come a long way from the days when "spare the rod, spoil the child" was the mantra of both parenting and schooling. At best, punishment will teach kids what not to do, which doesn't seem very useful as a way to get them to learn new things.

But that antipunishment attitude changes when we talk, not about individual children, but about institutions, about schools and districts that don't make adequate yearly progress (AYP) for all groups of students. Nearly everyone condones the use of sanctions (i.e., punishments) to discipline underperforming schools. Surely one way to get teachers and administrators to improve the education they deliver is to tell them that, if test scores don't improve, the students will be allowed to transfer out or get private tutoring at the school's expense— both sanctions NCLB imposes. Ultimately, if all else fails, the school will be taken apart and remade, with a new principal and many new staff members. That should shake 'em up. How much more serious can it get?

The Obama administration's "blueprint" is long on vague rhetoric and short on details, in part because it has only begun to work its way through the sausage-grinder of congressional committees, but it still creates "reward" schools and "challenge" schools. The former are to be rewarded for producing improvements in test scores and other measures; the latter will be "challenged" by being required to adopt specified "turnaround" strategies as well as to accept staffing changes, offer school choice, and work with outside organizations. A list of "interventions" not entirely unlike NCLB's sanctions. Details, presumably, will be forthcoming as policy makers examine our schools through their behaviorist lenses.

But we submit that, by and large, these strategies are just wishful thinking and a prime example of what Kohn terms "pop behaviorism." There's very little difference between sanctioning a school that fails to raise its test scores and withholding dessert from a child who fails to eat his vegetables. Of course, the child won't need to hurt himself to comply, while the school just might.

But surely the strategy of improving schools through the use of punishments and rewards must work or entire federal programs wouldn't be built on it? Maybe not. Writing in the *Journal of Law and Education*, Alex Duran summarizes the goals of the sanctions in NCLB and argues:

> The use of sanctions and consequences is intended to create incentives for schools that do not make AYP to undergo reform efforts that produce significant, sustained, and continued improvements in the academic achievement of their students for fear of losing federal funding or losing authority to manage and operate their schools. Unfortunately, *the prescribed sanctions and consequences are not based on empirical evidence* that clarifies and justifies the effectiveness of their use, which creates concerns toward their validity. Once again, the process of validation is complex as researchers acknowledge the difficulty of interpretations for an observed score and the even greater difficulties associated with reaching consensus on the appropriate uses of test scores in applied contexts. Recognizing differences in school context is a first step toward understanding the unique set of challenges that individual schools encounter.[3] (Emphasis added.)

But our quid pro quo accountability programs don't take any account of the "unique set of challenges" that confront individual schools. These challenges vary according to the poverty level and demographics of the school community. How much a school can accomplish with its young charges depends more than a little bit on how strong a social support system the families and community can provide. Failing to take account of these differences is like never noticing that the butcher had his thumb on the scale when he weighed your roast.

When we look at some of the studies of sanctions in the accountability programs of individual states, we find that the researchers make only very limited claims about how effective the sanctions are. And even in some of those cases, the findings are easily overstated.

In the days before NCLB, Heinrich Mintrop looked at a sample of schools in Kentucky and Maryland that had been put on academic probation. Those states had reasonably innovative performance assessment systems at the time, so his analysis is more a critique of the effectiveness of the sanction than of the kind of testing used. One positive finding from his study is that school staffs are always moved to take some kind of action when their school is placed on probation. It's a wake-up call. Everyone on the staff knows that there is work to do, and Mintrop's study found that schools can sometimes arrest a decline in test scores, at least temporarily. They do so by dint of a great deal of additional hard work on those activities that best raise test scores. As we showed in chapters 2 and 3, though, that means a focus on the narrow sample of skills most likely to be tested and on the specific ways of thinking that the test setting encourages.

So in this case the sanction of being on probation is like the two-by-four the farmer uses to bash his mule over the head to get its attention. Surely those who adopted the probation policy intended it to mean more. But what more? Mintrop continues:

> Probation did instill in schools the notion that "something" had to be done, but in none of the schools did probation trigger elements of internal accountability, if this is to mean a process through which a faculty formulates its own expectations in light of student needs and high demands of the system, agrees upon formal structures that hold them to account, and focuses improvement on identified key instructional deficiencies.

Being sanctioned doesn't do anything to create that all-important internal accountability and turns out to be little more than the farmer's two-by-four over the head. Neither does being sanctioned tell a staff what is wrong or how to go about improving the situation, and the schools most likely to be sanctioned are those that serve the rural and urban poor, the very schools most likely to have difficulty getting and keeping a top-flight staff in the first place. Mintrop highlights this obvious downside:

> But pressure is a double-edged sword. It may challenge people to increase work effort, but also make them want to leave if they do not value the pressure as serving a worthy purpose. Increasing pressure would have exacerbated the already immense problem of job commitment in the studied schools.[4]

So while being singled out for sanctions might focus a school staff's attention for a time, it gives merely the illusion of improvement. Extraordinary efforts at test preparation may halt or even temporarily reverse a decline in scores, but unless "internal accountability" exists—and the sanctions have nothing to do with creating that—real instructional improvement isn't likely to occur.

As to the tendency to overstate findings, Damien Betebenner analyzed a 2007 study of the lowest-performing schools in Florida's A+ accountability program, that state's NCLB testing program, complete with the required array of sanctions. These low-performing schools had received grades of F. The authors of the original study sought to show that a causal connection existed between subsequent achievement gains in these low-performing schools and the sanctions imposed on them by Florida's accountability system. When they found statistically significant connections between gains and sanctions in some schools, they inferred a causal connection. Betebenner commends them for using a comprehensive set of data and for trying to isolate the impact of the program from a great deal of surrounding statistical noise. But Betebenner's overall conclusion is that the authors did not succeed in showing that the sanctions "caused" the later improvement in any of these schools.[5]

But we can almost hear you asking as you read, "Those are sanctions, punishments. You know, *negative* reinforcements, and we agree they're not good. What about rewards? What about *positive* reinforcements? Shouldn't we be using them to motivate schools to improve?" First, while they are indeed punishments, they are not negative reinforcements.[6] But, language aside, you wouldn't be alone in thinking this way. Let's take as our text a passage from a report to the U.S. Department of Education from the Mid-Atlantic Regional Advisory Committee. It begins by considering sanctions:

> NCLB imposes a series of sanctions on schools in districts that fail to make their adequate yearly progress (AYP) goals. NCLB also requires education leaders to use research-based data in guiding their intervention decisions. Currently there are no readily available studies (perhaps because they don't exist) on the effectiveness of sanctions or on effective ways of dealing with sanctions.[7]

That passage starkly reiterates the point we've made that we lack evidence that the sanctions imposed by federal law will work as our leaders intend. But there's more. In the next sentence, the report adds, "Also, NCLB includes sanctions but no incentive to motivate change. A system with all sticks and no carrots is difficult to manage." That seems sensible, but would a system that includes carrots work better? We've almost always mentioned rewards in the same disparaging breath as punishments, just as if they were both somehow misguided. And we believe that the evidence suggests that they usually are.

WHAT ABOUT REWARDS?

After reviewing a good deal of the research that demonstrates that rewards aren't very effective at getting people to do what we want them to, Alfie Kohn lays out five reasons that rewards don't work. The first four he treats in a chapter aptly titled "The Trouble with Carrots." They are: rewards punish, rewards rupture relationships, rewards ignore reasons, and rewards discourage risk taking. Some of these reasons are easier to accept than others, though all are derived from research, but the fifth reason, to which Kohn devotes an entire chapter, is titled "Cutting the Interest Rate," and it makes the argument that rewards dampen interest in and enthusiasm for the activity that is rewarded.[8]

Wait just a minute now! There must be something wrong. That last one doesn't seem to make any sense at all. We know it's counterintuitive for most people, and we felt the same way when we first heard it, too. The idea that rewards motivate without doing any harm is deeply ingrained in popular culture. But there's a long line of studies that undercut this belief. A good review of these studies was conducted by Edward Deci and his colleagues.[9] One of the classic studies, now more than thirty years old, has been replicated in other settings, with different age students, and with different types of rewards. We'll quote Daniel Willingham, a cognitive psychologist at the University of Virginia, whose retelling of the original study appeared in one of his "Ask the Cognitive Scientist" columns for *The American Teacher*. His overall take on rewards is somewhat less negative than Kohn's, but the findings of the study he reports here are robust:

Children (aged 3 to 5 years old) were surreptitiously observed in a classroom with lots of different activities available. The experimenters noted how much time each child spent drawing with markers. The markers were then unavailable to students for two weeks. At the end of the two weeks, students were broken into three groups. Each student in the first group was taken to a separate room and was told that he or she could win an attractive "Good Player" certificate by drawing a picture with the markers. Each was eager to get the certificate and drew a picture. One-by-one, students in a second group were also brought to a separate room, encouraged to draw, and then given a certificate, but the certificate came as a surprise; when they started drawing, they didn't know that they would get the certificate. A third group of students served as a control group. They had been observed in the first session but didn't draw or get a certificate in this second session. After another delay of about two weeks, the markers again appeared in the classroom, and the experimenters observed how much children used them. The students in the first group—those who were promised the certificate for drawing—used the markers about half as much as students in the other two groups. Promising and then giving a reward made children like the markers less. But giving the reward as a surprise (as with the second group) had no effect.[10]

Willingham, perhaps in a compromise with current practice, recognizes that rewards can work for limited purposes, but he likens their use to taking out a loan: "You get an immediate benefit, but you will eventually have to pay up, with interest." So he recommends, first, looking for an alternative; then, using rewards for a specific purpose only, not as a general strategy; and finally, having a plan for ending them.

Where standardized testing for accountability is concerned, we don't have to worry too much about the reward side of the reward/punishment balance because we haven't been dangling a great many rewards in front of kids. And from what we've said in this chapter, that's probably not a bad thing.[11]

WORTH WORKING FOR?

But what about teachers? Shouldn't we encourage them to work harder by paying them more? Isn't that the way it's done in business? And aren't test scores our best means of sorting out the good teachers from the bad? There is more than a coincidental connection between the ways we usually try to "fix" our schools and the quick fixes we resort to when we want to improve the productivity of our workforce, whether in education or in business. As Sharon Nichols and David Berliner point out, "Accountability in education is modeled on corporate efforts to increase productivity."[12] You'll even hear the word *productivity* tossed around in discussions of schools, though it's always a bit muddy as to just what the schools are supposed to be producing.[13] But if the product of schools is seen to be test scores, we have to wonder where exactly the market for them is located.

While scores on standardized tests are usually taken as a measure of a school's productivity, even the truest believers in the standards and testing movement will admit when pressed that these scores are at best a proxy for the *learning* that schools are supposed to produce. We've argued that the tests are, in fact, pretty poor measures of that learning, but we maintain even more strongly that such academic learning is only part of what we want our schools to do. We want our schools to produce citizens, ready to begin their working lives or their higher educations, but also ready to assume their place in society, to govern themselves, and to live with their neighbors in a democratic society. While the academic skills students acquire are one important means of enabling kids to reach these broader goals, the skills acquired—even if you accept the imperfect measures of them—are by no means the only goal of our schools. We touched on the matter of purpose in chapter 1 and will delve deeper in chapter 11.

Clearly, schools and businesses differ in lots of ways. It would be pointless to catalogue all of them here. Just a couple should make the point. Everyone needs money (wages) to survive; no one actually needs grades or test scores to survive, as demonstrated by those schools that have done away with letter grades and the hundreds of colleges that have become admission-test optional.[14] And consider for a moment what happens to a student who causes

problems for others in school and what might happen to a worker who did the
same on the job. A very different outcome would be certain.

But schools are also workplaces for teachers and others, and one thing that
is the same about most of our schools and businesses is the dominance of the
behaviorist model of accountability. This model—all rewards and punishments, all the time—is endemic to both settings: set goals, measure progress
toward meeting them, reward the successful, and punish (make that sanction)
the unsuccessful. But that model, for all its simplicity, misunderstands both
industrial workers and teachers.

The issue comes down to answering two questions:

- Why do people work?
- Why do they work well?

One of the primary reasons workers work is for a paycheck; everyone
needs money to survive. So dangling more payroll carrots in front of workers
should make them work harder and better, no? No. It's been known for decades that while workers certainly work for a paycheck, they don't work *better* merely for additional pay. To understand this seeming paradox, consider
that W. Edwards Deming went on record many times with the reminder that
"pay is not a motivator." However, it can be a *de*motivator.[15]

If that seems puzzling at first, here's an explanation from Frederick Herzberg, the originator of this distinction. Herzberg's insight, now fifty years old,
divides the things people find motivating about their work into two categories: "motivating" factors, which include things like sense of achievement,
recognition, and interesting work; and "hygiene" factors, which are things
like pay, working conditions, and kinds of supervision. Once your working
conditions or salary reach a threshold that seems fair and meets your liveli-
hood needs, going higher may be nice, but it won't cause you to work harder
or better. Your intrinsic interest in the work or increased job responsibilities
will be what motivates you to continue to work harder and strive to improve.

The idea that rewards can be *de*motivators should be even more troubling
in professional fields, such as teaching, where the work itself is intrinsically
motivating. If the research shows that interest in a task declines most for those
who initially liked and were engaged by the task (remember the kids with
the markers), then a simple quid pro quo arrangement for educators—give us
better test scores and we'll give you more money—is apt to be doomed from
the start. Look at what Donald Gratz, one of the designers of a pilot pay-for-
performance plan in Denver, had to say:

[T]he failure of test-based pay for performance as a workable concept in
education comes down to a few primary points. The first is that the strategies

that work best for measurement—for measuring student progress fairly and accurately across many classrooms and schools—undercut good educational practice. Conversely, the strategies that work best for actually increasing student learning are not appropriate for comparative measurement. This was shown 300 years ago by the British experience and has been shown once again in Denver.[16]

Three hundred years ago? Yes, we've been at this game of trying to get people to perform the way we want them to for a very long time, and our track record isn't all that good. Gratz reminds us that as early as 1710, teachers' salaries in parts of England "were based on their children's scores on examinations in reading, writing, and arithmetic."[17] What's more, Gratz's view of the Denver plan is not negative. He believes that the collaboration that went into designing Denver's accountability plan will ultimately yield a design that will be based on a mix of professional judgment, contribution to the overall good, and various subjective and objective measures. (Yes, unlike us, but like most common usage, Gratz applies the word *objective* to standardized tests.)

The takeaway message from this chapter is simply this: people are not pigeons. Whether they're children in school, teachers in the classroom, or workers in industry, the simple-minded application of rewards and punishments doesn't work the way many people believe it should. Human motivation is far more complex and understood far less well than that of a starving pigeon. (Yes, the pigeons and rats used in the behaviorist experiments were kept very hungry, if not quite at death's door.) When we humans decide to do something—study hard to learn in a specific discipline, for example—our motives include all sorts of familial, cultural, and social factors, not just a simple calculus of what's in it for us.

To the extent that we can make people take part in the carrot-and-stick game of rewards and punishments, we run smack into some nasty unintended consequences. When children in school become focused on rewards, their interest in the learning task diminishes; when workers become focused on bonuses, competition, and pay scales in general, so does their interest in their jobs; when teachers focus on the connection of their students' test scores to their own salaries, they begin to lose their enthusiasm for their calling. The reasons are basically the same. Call people's attention to things other than the task at hand—whether making widgets, selling cars, or learning to read—and you distract them from the task itself.

Such unintended consequences are not uncommon where testing is concerned. In the next chapter, we take up a special case of inadvertently directing attention to the wrong things as we spend some time exploring Campbell's Law.

Testing Autobiography: Joan's Story

The tests had no impact on my own educational history. But unlike Phil, I didn't begin to question the tests because of any peculiar research findings. I began to observe the negative impact that the tests were having on the kids in my own classroom.

I began my career as a Title I teacher, working on reading with small groups of first- and second-graders who had qualified for the special assistance based primarily on their low family income. Students who were identified as needing extra help were pulled out of regular classes and sent to me, the Title I reading teacher, for supplemental instruction.

Part of the law that established Title I (the Elementary and Secondary Education Act of 1965) was a requirement that students be tested regularly. This was seen as a way to ensure that the federal funds were being spent as Congress intended. But we also used the results to help diagnose student deficiencies. At the time, testing seemed to me like a perfectly sensible way to do that.

When a position opened in the district for a regular first-grade classroom teacher, I applied and was hired. In that very year, a statewide program of testing all students in all grades began. Predictably, it was a disaster for the youngest children, and after that year, statewide testing was abandoned for first and second grades.

When I began teaching third grade in a different school in the same district, statewide testing was already becoming a yearly expectation, and it included third grade. However, because the test was given in the spring, teachers were unable to even try to use the results for diagnosis and remediation, except for determining a student's eligibility for summer school.

The spring administration continued for a few years, but the state moved the testing to a September date in the hope that the results would be ready soon enough to allow teachers time to develop remediation plans for the small number of students who didn't meet the state standard.

Once the testing was moved to the fall, teachers were somewhat insulated from any effort to hold them directly responsible for their students' test scores. They just didn't have much of a chance to teach at all before the testing date.

Today, the test date has been moved back to the spring, and the current federal administration, through such efforts as its new Race to the Top program, seems determined to evaluate teachers based on their students' standardized test scores. This, too, will lead to unintended negative consequences if for no other reason than this: *attendance is compulsory; learning is voluntary.*

While the tests have not yet become a teacher's official "report card," their influence has been felt in many areas. Under the fall testing plan, teachers were responsible for developing remediation plans for students who didn't meet the standard. They were required to meet with parents of students who fell below the state's cut score and inform them that their child would need remediation during the year, might have to attend summer school, or might even be held back and not promoted. Because ours was not a Title I school, which required a specific percentage of students to qualify for the federal program, we lacked any supplemental help, and teachers had to develop their own remediation plans. Fortunately, we were able to enlist the help of parents and Indiana University students in carrying out the plans we developed.

Over the years I began to notice some troubling aspects about the way the test scores were being used. Scores known as "cut scores" (see glossary), which were used for summer school eligibility, changed from year to year, sometimes by a lot. I never got a straight answer to questions I raised about these changes—not an official answer anyway. However, a friend at the state department informed me that cut scores were determined at least partly according to the amount of money the state had available to fund summer school. I found that information both personally and professionally disappointing, and this led me to question other aspects of the way the tests were used.

My disappointment only increased when the local scores began to appear in newspapers where schools that differed considerably in terms of the socioeconomic status and ethnicity of their students were ranked according to average test scores. A few key individuals and some members of the press, especially editorial writers, began to claim that the test scores proved that schools and teachers were failing. Blaming teachers for their students' scores didn't seem to make any more sense to me than threatening children with retention because their scores fell below a cut score that had been set because of available funds.

Because these numbers were having an ever-growing impact on the students and their families, I thought I had better inform myself about the tests and start paying closer attention to the impact that the testing programs were having. In this way, I could help students and their parents understand that these test scores were not absolute or infallible and neither were the decisions made as a result.

I now look on the state assessment and other standardized tests as not simply a nuisance or a minor inconvenience. I believe they are doing more harm than good and that the millions spent on the testing could be put to better use in other ways, such as reducing class size (which we know makes a difference) and improving professional development for teachers. What's more, the time taken from instruction to prepare for the tests, to actually administer them, and to follow up on the results is simply not worth it. My estimate is that in the 2008–2009 school year, my students and I gave up a total of twenty days of learning time for test-related activities. Twenty days!

In addition, I often observed that the test scores did not match what I was seeing every day in the classroom. Many students who performed well on grade-level work in the classroom didn't show that same accomplishment on the tests. Some didn't test well; others were not feeling well or were having a bad day for other reasons, including emotional ones. (And students' emotions ran from fear, apprehension, and nervousness to boredom for those who expected to perform well.) But none of those reasons mattered when the test scores were handed down. We would admonish parents to see that their children had a good night's sleep, ate a good breakfast, and had an emotionally calm evening before and morning of the test. But we couldn't guarantee that any of those conditions would be true for any particular child. But that didn't matter either.

So I have worked to find better ways than test scores to inform parents about their child's performance. We're told that the tests are designed to tell us whether or not children are learning, but open lines of communication among teachers, children, and parents are a far better way. To borrow some jargon from the testers, the conferences are more *valid* for individual kids than any of the tests, and the conferences lead directly to a plan for future learning. You can *rely* on it.

6

The Distortions of High Stakes

> When test scores go up, it is likely that the inference will be that better instruction is taking place . . . but this is not necessarily so.
>
> —Sharon Nichols and David Berliner, 2007

It's not soup . . . and it's not very comforting. But it is every bit as good at what it does as your grandmother's chicken soup is in helping you through a cold. We're talking about what social scientists have dubbed Campbell's Law, and it is responsible for much of the unintended mischief that occurs in the name of standardized testing. In 1975, Donald Campbell, a social psychologist, formally stated the law that now bears his name: "The more any quantitative social indicator is used for social decision-making, the more subject it will be to corruption pressures and the more apt it will be to distort and corrupt the social processes it was intended to monitor."[1] You can easily see how the high stakes currently attached to standardized testing in the United States would bring this law into play.

In chapter 5, we looked at the counterintuitive notion that rewards and punishments are counterproductive. When we use them to motivate complex behaviors, punishments and rewards not only don't do what we hope, they work against our hopes. By distracting the attention of students (and teachers) from the intrinsic interest of a task, these behaviorist schemes unintentionally lead them to undervalue the task itself. In the end, the task is done less willingly and less well. And in an even more troubling consequence, students will show less interest in the task in the future. While this outcome is surely unintended, reliance on rewards and punishments actually stunts these individuals' future development.

But what happens when our behaviorist impulses get the better of us, and we turn up the pressure in a big way by attaching high stakes—serious consequences, good or bad—to the outcomes of an assessment? What happens to the overall validity of the assessment system? What does the increased pressure do to individual learners? to teachers and administrators? to parents? to a community that finds itself under assault from federal rule makers? The basic assumption underlying standardized testing that we're taking up in this chapter is: *If the stakes attached to a test are made high enough, people will work harder and improve their performance on the task at hand.*

Campbell's Law, of course, suggests otherwise. The higher the stakes and the more we care about them, the less we can depend on the validity of the measurements we use. Clearly, this is a case of unintended consequences, and we'll be examining some specific cases in this chapter. But Campbell's Law applies to more than just the test scores and includes any of the array of "quantitative measures" derived from test scores, such as graduation rates, progress scores, or proficiency rates. If it's a number and something really important depends on it, we'll work hard, all right. But in working to gain the reward or avoid the penalty, we will subvert the accuracy of the measurement system. Moreover, when the stakes attached to a test score rise, people will surely work to raise that test score, but they won't necessarily focus on improving their performance on the task at hand.

If Alfie Kohn's *Punished by Rewards* was the foundation on which we built many of the arguments we mustered against a simple-minded behaviorism in the preceding chapter, *Collateral Damage*, by Sharon Nichols and David Berliner, fills that role in this chapter.[2] The book was published in 2007, so naturally the authors' primary focus is the No Child Left Behind (NCLB) Act.

However, the use of high stakes to drive human activities didn't begin with NCLB and its successor, the Obama "blueprint," which does little to alter the high-stakes model of education reform. High stakes have been attached to indicators in areas other than education—with exactly the disappointing results that Campbell's Law predicts. We don't need to look further for examples than the dismal financial news of the past few years—even before the financial meltdown of 2008–2009. A company's stock price is supposed to reflect its intrinsic value, as the market prices it. When it does so, the indicator is doing its job. When executive bonuses are tied to that stock price, however, executives will work very hard indeed, which can mean cutting staff, selling less profitable but solid pieces of the corporation, and taking any number of steps designed to raise the stock price—and with it their bonuses. When the stock price rises as a result of such actions, its validity as a good indicator of the value of the company is diminished. The indicator has been corrupted.

Although we've argued *against* the assumptions that standardized tests and their cut scores are objective and that the sliver of content measured is enough to enable us to make useful and valid inferences about something as broad as student achievement, let's set aside those arguments—at least for this chapter. Let's conduct a thought experiment and consider the fictional ideal world inhabited by the true believers in the basic assumptions we've dealt with so far. In that ideal world, the tests and their construction are absolutely objective. They are normed (see the glossary for a definition of norm-referencing) on good and demographically representative samples of students. And they include enough well-designed questions to allow us to draw sound inferences about student performance.

Then one day, into this psychometric paradise come those officials who dole out the rewards and impose the punishments, all in the name of motivating educators and students to work harder. Moreover, these are stringent sanctions and valuable rewards: that is, the stakes are high. For students, high stakes can mean things like receiving a high school diploma or not, being promoted to the next grade or not, or being required to attend summer school or not. For teachers and administrators high stakes can mean a range of things from getting a significant bonus when scores go up, to having a state-appointed administrator take over a school when they go down, to the firing and reconstituting of the entire staff of a school when low scores continue to slip. This is serious stuff.

We argued in chapter 5 that rewards and sanctions don't work as motivators and can even be counterproductive. But setting that point aside for the moment, when those consequences are distributed according to the dictates of some quantitative measure—and you can't get much more quantitative than a test score—what happens to the accuracy of the measure? (Remember, we're granting all the validity and reliability to the measurement that its most ardent supporters could wish for.) According to Campbell's Law, the measure becomes corrupted. That is, the inferences you are able to draw from the measure are less valid.

For example, if a test is designed to measure students' learning of, say, fourth-grade mathematics, but the test preparation is excessive, the tested students will no longer be comparable to the group on which the test was normed. Or if a teacher uses information from state guidelines or from experience with previous years' tests or—in rare cases—even gets a look at copies of the test in advance and creates a set of test-prep exercises for her students, their familiarity with the format and likely content of the test will also make them different from the group of students on which the test was normed. In such cases, even the scores on our ideally designed and constructed—and wholly hypothetical—test would no longer be accurate measures of student learning.

And that's what's been happening in our high-stakes-test-driven world. Nichols and Berliner devote their entire book to the way these most unintended of consequences of our current high-stakes accountability system have been playing out. But in this single chapter we want to focus in particular on four areas because the problems they represent are widespread and, with one exception, are not widely known to the general public or to educators and parents. Thus they are not widely discussed. These unintended consequences are cheating (the one that's widely reported), the dropout/pushout rates, the "bubble kids," and the narrowed curriculum.

CHEATING

Campbell's Law is quite clear that "indicators" are corrupted—meaning that they no longer do a very good job of measuring performance. But the people in a system driven by high-stakes testing can be corrupted as well. Nichols and Berliner devote a good deal of space to citing examples of the kind of cheating that teachers and administrators resort to under the pressure of high-stakes accountability systems.[3] Indeed, the authors express some sympathy for those educators caught up in an assessment system that strikes many people as unfair.

The examples Nichols and Berliner cite fall along a moral continuum—from least troubling to most egregious. How would you judge a teacher who, having seen the previous year's exam, works to design practice problems for his students that are very similar to—but not copies of—the items used on the previous test and are quite likely to appear in similar form again? Is that even cheating? Maybe not, but it certainly undercuts the validity of any decisions that might be made as a result of his students' subsequent test scores. The norming group—the students against whose original performance his students will be judged—didn't have this kind of preparation.

How is what that teacher is doing different from what high school students do when they take one of the popular SAT-preparation courses? It's not really different at all, and to the extent that students "prep" for the SAT, they undercut its validity as a predictor of first-year college grades—which is all it was ever designed to do. The group on which the SAT was normed didn't get special practice on how to find main ideas and locate supporting details in brief, disconnected prose passages. Nor did they practice eliminating obviously wrong responses and adopting an informed guessing strategy. Yet those who take the preparation classes learn these and other techniques that serve to raise scores without making them better readers or better problem solvers—thus corrupting the indicator without improving the target behaviors.

Moving along the moral continuum, how would you judge a teacher who taps a student on the shoulder—but says nothing—as she points out that he has gotten off track on his answer sheet to the math section of the test and so is filling in the bubble for question number 10 when he's actually working on number 8? Strictly speaking, of course, she's cheating, and it's certainly "wrong" in the sense that it, too, messes up the validity of the test.

But let's complicate matters even further. Now suppose the youngster in question is a really good student who would easily score far above the proficiency level but for the "clerical" error he's making on his answer sheet? Certainly, the teacher's action is still cheating, but now, in addition to preventing the test from harvesting incorrect information about this student's performance, the teacher's action also helps the school benefit from his score, which is likely to be a high one. And the school might well need that high score to raise its average and so avoid sanctions. How reprehensible is this teacher's behavior?

To further muddy the waters, suppose a different student makes the same "clerical error" but has very low self-esteem when it comes to math and would really be set back by failing another test. What now? After all, we're only talking about what basketball referees call a "correctable error," like resetting the shot clock after viewing the TV monitor. Is the teacher right to do what she did? It seems we don't live in a simple world.

If we decide to hold the teachers in these examples fully responsible for their "cheating," what do we do with principals (and there have been a number of cases) who change answer sheets by erasing wrong answers and substituting correct ones? Now such a case probably provokes a range of emotions, from disappointment to anger. And the truth is that no one really knows how prevalent the problem is for we only know about the cases that have come to light. But it's probably true that for every case like the answer-changing principal, which seems clearly wrong on every level, you can come up with at least as many cases of the compassionate teacher who believes the test and the situation unfairly disadvantage her students.

The problem of cheating by adults has become big enough that anyone with a browser and a good Internet connection can turn up examples, one after another. Even the economists who study social trends have begun researching the issue. In a 2004 issue of *Education Next*, a publication of the conservative Hoover Institution, economists Brian Jacob and Steven Levitt report their analyses of ways to single out instances of cheating (http://pricetheory. uchicago.edu/levitt/Academics.html). They offer among their conclusions:

As might be expected, the cheating by school personnel increased following the introduction of high-stakes testing, particularly in the lowest-performing classrooms. For example, the likelihood of cheating in a classroom that was one standard deviation below the mean increased by roughly 29% in response to the school probation policy and 43% due to the ending of social promotion.[4]

However, they conclude that explicit cheating by school personnel "is not likely to be a serious enough problem by itself to call into question high-stakes testing, both because the most egregious forms of cheating are relatively rare and, more important, because cheating could be virtually eliminated at a relatively low cost through the implementation of proper safeguards."[5] They go on to explain that other, subtler forms of cheating, such as some kinds of test preparation, may be harder to detect but ought not to deter educators and policy makers from the challenge "to develop a system that captures the obvious benefits of high-stakes testing as a means of providing incentives while minimizing the possible distortions that these measures induce."[6] Obvious benefits? Despite the success of Levitt's two best-selling books, *Freakonomics* and its successor *Superfreakonomics*, his analysis might be improved if he acknowledged the "obvious disadvantages" of these kinds of incentives. And we would remind Levitt and all of his coauthors that Campbell's Law has not been repealed, which makes minimizing the "possible distortions" unlikely.

And how would you minimize the distortion, cited by Nichols and Berliner, that took place in the Birmingham, Alabama, schools in 2000? And remember, this took place before No Child Left Behind. In Birmingham, school officials had 522 students "administratively withdrawn" just before the annual high-stakes exams were administered.[7] Predictably, the district's scores rose, and perhaps also predictably, the superintendent got a nice bonus for beating expectations. How are these school officials different from, say, Bernie Madoff, whose elaborate Ponzi scheme duped even the most supposedly savvy investors? Right. These so-called educators have even *lower* moral standards. At least Madoff messed with adults, who might have figured out what he was up to if they tried and made a run for the exit. But these school officials were messing with children—and the most vulnerable children at that. The good news for educators' ethics is that it was an adult education teacher who noticed all the kids newly dumped from the school system who were showing up in his classes just before test time. He blew the whistle. Bravo! And he was fired.

The problems don't seem likely to get better, at least not as long as our system of school accountability is tied closely to the high-stakes-attached test scores. And the examples keep on coming. In June 2008, online columnist Jacquie McTaggart of *EdNews* quoted the following tidbit from a 2007 *San*

Francisco Chronicle story, which included numerous examples of teachers
and administrators behaving badly, even if their motives were good:

> Principal Alene Wheaton of Muir Elementary in San Francisco discovered and re-
> ported the unique method for administering "standardized" tests employed by one of
> her third-grade teachers: Students answered questions on scratch paper, the teacher
> corrected them, and the students transferred the right answers to the test booklet.[8]

That's not the kind of "small distortion" that's easy to fix, and it doesn't
take an economist to see what impact this teacher has on the validity of the
tests her students take.

DROPOUTS/PUSHOUTS

While cheating by educators might or might not be common—there are no
reliable national figures—at least the examples that do come to light are
fairly easy to explain. Nothing about the problem of dropouts (or pushouts)
is simple, except for the fact that dropping out of school is a bad thing for
almost everyone who does it.

For those of you who might have paused on the term *pushout*, it refers to
students who drop out of school after having been "encouraged" to do so by
school officials. Now no school has an assistant principal for pushing low-
achieving or troublesome students (sometimes the same ones) out the door.
But there are ways. Sometimes a student will be counseled out of the regular
high school into a GED (high school equivalency) program, which allows the
school to remove the student from its roles without counting him or her as a
dropout.[9] And don't be misled by a school's claim to be "award winning." A
few well-chosen policy changes can make a school's quantitative indicators—
things like graduation rate and attendance rate—look much better.[10] In addition, retention policies can hold students back so long that they are seriously
overage for the classes they attend, and many of these students ultimately drop
out. Did the retention policy play a role? You bet it did.[11]

Now, we certainly don't plan to open the mammoth can of worms labeled
"dropout rate," but if the term means anything, it should take account of
students who earn a GED credential. We think they ought to be counted as
graduates, even if they earn the credential in their early twenties. If that is the
case, the percentage of graduates stands in the low-to-mid eighties.[12] Otherwise, it was about 71 percent in 2008.[13] Not everyone agrees with us about
including GED holders as graduates, but whichever way you lean, we think
everyone will agree that there's something wrong with just ignoring kids

who are counseled into GED programs. Once again, Campbell's Law rears its head when the graduation rate (the indicator) is held to be more important than what it measures. The indicator then becomes corrupted and no longer provides a fair description of reality. Most of the graduation rates you read in the newspapers are political statements, not research reports.

BUBBLE KIDS

Like many of the examples of Campbell's Law at work, this one is another case of good intentions gone awry, and it has nothing to do with those unfortunate children born with seriously deficient immune systems who must be kept from the world's germs by a plastic bubble. This term is borrowed from the sports world. In one sense, it refers to racecar drivers who have barely made it into the field of the Indianapolis 500 and can be bumped during the late qualifying runs and are said to be "on the bubble." But the closest match to its use in education would be those college basketball teams that are very close to making the NCAA tournament. These teams need just a nudge, perhaps one more high-quality win, to "make it to the dance." Like those teams, kids who are very close to passing a high-stakes test are said to be "on the bubble."

When the stakes for a test are high—high school graduation, retention in grade, teachers and administrators' salaries and job security—the natural inclination of educators is to focus on what they can realistically achieve to earn the reward or avoid the sanction. And so educators will naturally focus on the needs of those students who are very close to passing a high-stakes test—in other words, the bubble kids. This can mean such things as giving extra help in class to these bubble kids (individually or in small groups), holding special tutoring sessions with them throughout the day or after school or on weekends, creating special summer school programs for them, and using specialist teachers (librarians, gym teachers, etc.) as test-prep tutors for the bubble kids instead of having them teach their regular subjects.[14]

The problem is real, it's national, and it's ongoing. The Center for Education Policy (CEP), a nonpartisan research and policy analysis group, has been reporting on the impact of assessment and accountability policies around the nation for a number of years. A recent CEP release in this area notes that Rhode Island teachers know the term and use it when describing how they focus on the bubble kids:

> In five of the six Rhode Island schools studied, interviewees discussed how they strategically targeted resources and interventions on the "bubble kids"—those scoring just below the proficient level on state tests—in an attempt to

raise their scores to proficient. Interviewees in Illinois also spoke about the same general trend.[15]

But all of this extra attention to the kids on the bubble means that educators must compromise some of their principles, which leads them to an ironic perversion of the literal meaning of the phrase "no child left behind." Instead of working assiduously to help all the children in their charge, educators feel pressed to engage in what amounts to "educational triage." The high achievers are left to fend for themselves; they can take care of themselves and will pass anyway. Meanwhile, the so-called hopeless cases, who have little chance of passing and find themselves mired at the bottom of the educational heap, are simply abandoned there.[16] They just have too far to climb to make it to proficiency in time for the test.

Now, in the imaginary world of this chapter—where the claims of the standardized test mongers are taken to be valid—what can we say about any test and its validity when educators focus their preparation on a small segment of the student population? That's right. It's no longer the stunningly accurate measuring stick it once was. The gains reported because a few kids were pushed above the test's cut score for proficiency are an artifact of bad educational practice. Still another distortion has been created by the devastating impact of attaching high stakes to test scores.

A NARROWED CURRICULUM

No matter how you slice it, when high stakes are attached to tests, lots of test preparation will take place. The recent CEP report on Rhode Island and Illinois reveals this clearly:

> In Rhode Island, many teachers and administrators specifically acknowledged the pressure to "teach to the test" by focusing curriculum on the specific content or skills likely to be tested. In Illinois, many teachers interviewed said they integrated test preparation into their instruction throughout the school year, but some noted that they could only teach more creative, broader-themed, or project-oriented lessons after the state test was given.[17]

We devote the next chapter ("What's Left Out?") to the subjects that have been shoehorned into the pockets of time that remain after all the testing and preparation in the "biggies" (reading/language arts and math) have been completed. Here we want to say just a few words about the test-prep activities that fill up the time taken away from nontested subjects, and we want you to think about that issue in terms of Campbell's Law.

When someone criticizes the schools for engaging in excessive test preparation, a common counterargument we've heard goes like this: If you have a good test, teaching to the test is not a bad thing.[18] Seems logical, but by now, we're betting you can predict what our response will be? That's right. We would say, "The test you have isn't good enough to teach to." And it isn't. But we're not allowed to say that here, because for this chapter we've agreed to accept the claims of the biggest fans of standardized testing. Even so, the high stakes that drive the test-preparation efforts of educators across the country will lead to a corrupted indicator. Nichols and Berliner put the problem this way:

> We've known for some time that as consequential tests approach, teachers increase their time in test preparation. Some of that is sensible. But under the high-stakes testing requirements of NCLB, it appears that much of that increased time is inappropriate, both bad for teachers and children and destructive of the very indicator that is used to measure student achievement.[19]

How does that work? How does the indicator get destroyed? When 80 percent of teachers report spending more than 20 percent of their time in test preparation and when 28 percent of teachers report spending more than 60 percent of their time preparing for the state tests, how accurate is the test's reading of student achievement?[20] Remember that the test is designed to give an estimate of the performance of your school's students in comparison to the group of students on which the test was normed. And that estimate depends on sound judgment by the test makers about what the curriculum looks like, about sampling the content of the curriculum, and about designing items to measure fairly students' knowledge of that content.

If the curriculum on paper looks a lot like the state's standards, that's to be expected. Theoretically, the test makers can use that information to help them sample the content. But when more than one-fourth of teachers are spending more than half their time on test preparation, we shouldn't be surprised at findings such as this one, again from the CEP:

> The study also found that teachers in schools identified for improvement under NCLB were less likely than those in higher-achieving schools to use a wider range of instructional practices, such as hands-on activities, student seat work, reading aloud, and learning centers.[21]

And the time saved from forgoing this wide range of activities goes directly into "drilling, emphasizing rote memorization, teaching students how to take tests, reviewing over and over again the concepts that will be represented on the test, and giving multiple practice tests."[22] When that happens the test is no longer the good measure of achievement (remember we're accepting this point of view temporarily) that it once was.

Let's consider a hypothetical case that might be a little too close to reality for some readers. Suppose a study of the investment industry determined that in successful brokerages, the traders made more trades than they did in less successful firms. So an investment bank introduced an incentive program that would give substantial monetary rewards to its brokers according to the number of sales transactions they completed during a month's time—not how profitable the transactions were for the company nor whether they made sense in the long-term plans of the clients. What do you think would happen?

One thing is certain: test scores would rise. No, wait, that's not quite right. Make that, the number of trades completed by the brokers would certainly rise. But would the bank be more successful? Without some other changes, that's not likely. The indicator would quickly become corrupted by the brokers' very reasonable actions. They might make a series of smaller transactions, for example, which would increase their numbers. They might churn some of their clients' holdings—trade them back and forth among themselves without really accomplishing the goals of growth and security for the clients. The next time an industry study was conducted, the corruption of the indicator would be well begun. No longer would number of trades be a good indicator of a successful firm.

Okay, we admit that the final hypothetical example is a little far-fetched. No reasonable person would think you could measure something as complex as the activity of an investment bank with an instrument as blunt as the number of transactions. It barely samples the broad domain of the brokers' activities; it isn't really a measure of the high quality of personal service we want from our brokers; the brokers can distort their activities to raise the scores on the indicator without really doing their clients any good; and attaching high stakes to so weak an indicator only brings Campbell's Law into play and leads to the corruption of the indicator.

But before you turn the page, try substituting "teacher" for "broker" and "test scores" for "number of transactions" in the that previous paragraph. Maybe the example isn't so far-fetched after all.

In chapter 7, we'll move from the way high-stakes testing can distort the indicators, the quantitative measures themselves, to its impact on curriculum and pedagogy, in lay terms, its effect on what's taught and how.

WITHIN LIMITS, TESTS CAN BE USEFUL,
STANLEY POGROW

First, students should not be penalized because other students are doing better. The tests should be used to see where students stand on some absolute basis. (It has been too easy to game the current comparative approach.)

Second, there should be a limit on how much time schools can spend teaching to the test or providing remedial help in the aftermath.

When these conditions apply, I have found standardized tests to be very predictive of actual student progress and very responsive to well-designed progressive approaches. The vast majority of progressive interventions and reforms fail to show gains on standardized tests, but much of the progressive antipathy toward standardized tests results from a gut suspicion about anything that is systematic (often for good reasons).

The problem is not the tests but the disorganization of most progressive initiatives. They tend to be long on ideals that I support, but short on details. This causes real problems in large-scale implementation. On the other hand, as a designer of progressive interventions, I have found that standardized tests are indeed highly predictive. Interventions such as the Higher Order Thinking Skills (HOTS) project and Supermath have always produced higher gains in standardized test scores than do simplistic approaches. However, that is probably because my programs are more structured than most progressive initiatives, and my research into the conditions of effectiveness enables me to adjust the intervention.

Stanley Pogrow, creator of the HOTS thinking skills curriculum, is a professor of Educational Leadership at San Francisco State University.

7

What's Left Out?

How many quarts are there in a bushel? In a gallon? In a half bushel?

—Country School Examinations, Winter Term 1913

Kipling wrote about filling the "unforgiving minute with sixty seconds worth of distance run." We always wondered if he had ever been a teacher. It's a simple fact of every elementary teacher's life that there are never enough hours in the week to fit in all the subjects and topics that children should be learning about at a depth that will engage their curious minds. Secondary teachers face a similar squeeze, though for them the competition for time takes place among topics within a single discipline. But in both cases, time in school is a zero-sum game: If you add something to a teacher's plate, you have to take something away. If not, something else will be pushed out that you might not want to lose.

One popular option for dealing with the limited time during the school day has always been for teachers to focus in-depth on one or two areas within a subject and help students engage in deep exploration of those areas. In this view, learning to think like a scientist or to reason like a historian is more important than memorizing the component parts of a cell or stockpiling details about the Industrial Revolution. Depth of learning is seen as more important than breadth of coverage. The polar opposite position—sadly, the more popular—involves surveying entire fields of learning so as to "cover" the curriculum and "stuff kids like turkeys" with as much factual material as possible. In this view, covering all of the legislated curriculum—at least touching briefly on all of a state's standards—becomes the primary goal.

The battle between depth and coverage for the limited space in the school day has been a part of school life for a long time. Today, however, the spread of high-stakes standardized testing has changed the ground on which the battle is fought. With the proliferation of state-level standards whose attainment the tests are supposed to assess, the balance has tipped in favor of coverage over depth. In order to sample a domain as broad as most sets of state standards, the test must skim the surface of the content, as we showed in chapter 2. And while that skimming affects the way content is covered in areas that are assessed, its impact is even starker on areas that are not assessed. The emphasis on skills in literacy and numeracy—on reading/language arts and math—has caused schools to direct time and resources to these areas at the expense of social studies, science, art and music, health and physical education, civic engagement, and personal development.[1]

The basic assumption about standardized tests that we're treating in this chapter is this: *Standardized tests simply measure whether students have learned content deemed important; the tests don't influence what's taught or how.* Our analysis falls naturally into two parts, captured by Monty Neill, executive director of the National Center for Fair and Open Testing, in an invited response he posted to the Freakonomics blog, which is housed at the *New York Times* website. Neill wrote: "High-stakes testing has narrowed and dumbed down curricula; eliminated time spent on untested subjects like social studies, art, and even recess; turned classrooms into little more than test preparation centers. . . ."[2] *Narrowed* and *dumbed down* are the operative words: The subjects tested come to dominate the classroom, and the way we teach those subjects grows ever more superficial, becoming more like the tests themselves.

NARROWED CURRICULA

Without a doubt, the best source of data on the instructional time devoted to specific subjects—especially in response to changes in the regimen of testing—is a series of reports produced by the nonpartisan Center on Education Policy (CEP) in Washington, D.C. Founded by former congressional staffer Jack Jennings, the CEP has been tracking the impact of No Child Left Behind since the law took effect in 2002. In 2007 CEP issued *Choices, Changes, and Challenges: Curriculum and Instruction in the NCLB Era*, by Jennifer McMurrer (www.cep-dc.org), which used data on 349 school districts to conclude that, since NCLB was enacted, 62 percent of districts had increased the amount of time spent in elementary school on English/language arts (ELA) and/or math. In addition, 44 percent of all districts had increased time for ELA and/or math while also cutting time in science, social studies, art and music, physical education, lunch, or recess. (Some districts seem to have "found" time to increase classroom time spent on ELA or math without cutting anything else. While better efficiency is the explanation most districts offer, in the zero-sum world of school time, we are skeptical that much very free time was ever just lying around.)

Then in February 2008, CEP issued a follow-up report that delved even deeper into the data.[3] Together, the original report and its follow-up reveal a major shift in instructional time in the elementary schools, toward ELA and math and away from, well, everything else. Table 7.1 from the follow-up report that shows changes in instructional time in those districts that said they had increased time in either ELA or math.

What can we see from the data presented here? One thing jumps out. Of the four academic areas (excluding lunch and recess), each has experienced about a one-third decrease in instructional time since 2001–2002. That might not be a problem if we thought we had been spending too much time on these areas before. But does forty-five to fifty minutes a day for social studies or science seem excessive? We don't think so. Nor do we think that cutting forty to sixty minutes a week from art and music or from physical education and recess makes much sense either.

But the main point we want to make here is this: We don't remember being invited to the national discussion of the appropriate mix of subjects in our schools. Not only weren't we—or you—invited to such a discussion, we don't believe it ever took place. And that is a far more frightening prospect than whatever the outcome of such discussions might turn out to be. The absence of such talk—in school board meetings, in state legislatures, in newspapers, on TV and radio, on community blogs and websites—raises the question: Who is in charge here? We know in a democracy it's supposed to be the people, all of us collectively. But in this case, that just isn't so. We're asked to support testing policies, but we're not given the background material or the time to digest it that would enable us to make informed decisions.

We need to make one other point here about the subjects and activities that have been elbowed aside as the curriculum is hastily narrowed to make time for preparation in the subjects that are going to be on the test. Note that we referred to "academic" subjects and withheld comment on lunch and recess. But it's not because we don't think they are important. The CEP numbers on lunch are too small to enable the researchers to report their findings confidently, so we'll just comment on the reduction in recess. But since lunch involves getting up and moving around, socializing, and otherwise taking a break from the academic grind, it should offer benefits similar to those associated with recess.

Table 7.1. Changes since 2001–2002 in Instructional Time for Various Elementary School Subjects in Districts Reporting Decreases

Of those districts reporting an increase in instructional time for ELA and/or math AND a decrease in instructional time for one or more of the subjects listed . . .

Subject or Period	Average Total Instructional Time Pre-NCLB (Minutes per week)	Average Total Instructional Time Post-NCLB (Minutes per week)	Average Decrease (Minutes per week)	Average Decrease as a Percentage of Total Instructional Time
Social Studies	239	164	76	32%
Science	226	152	75	33%
Art and Music	154	100	57	35%
Physical Education	115	75	40	35%
Recess	184	144	50	28%
Lunch	*	*	*	*
One or more subjects listed	461	318	145	32%

Table reads: Among districts reporting an increase in instructional time for ELA and/or math and decreases for various subjects, the average total instructional time for social studies before NCLB was 239 minutes per week, compared with 164 minutes per week after NCLB. The average decrease for social studies was seventy-six minutes per week, or a 32 percent loss of time from the pre-NCLB level.

*Sample size was too small to allow reporting of data on minutes per week.

Note: More information about the calculations presented in this table can be found at www.cep-dc.org in the "Methodology" link accompanying this report.

Source: Center on Education Policy, February 2007, District Survey, Items 18 & 19 (table IT-188). Reproduced with permission.

Just what are kids missing when their recess time is reduced or cut out entirely? It could be a lot more than they're getting in exchange. In February 2009, a study appeared in the journal *Pediatrics* that, according to Tara Parker-Pope of the *New York Times*, "suggests that play and down time may be as important to a child's academic experience as reading, science, and math, and that regular recess, fitness or nature time can influence behavior, concentration, and even grades."[4] The researchers in this recent study analyzed data from a variety of sources on the performance of some 11,000 children. They found that those who had at least one fifteen-minute recess break a day were better behaved, judging by a variety of measures, than those who did not. Other studies have linked physical fitness and activity with academic achievement.[5]

Moreover, those children most likely to have little or no recess were also more likely to be black, to be from low-income families, and to be from large cities—the populations and locales where the most intense test preparation has become the norm. But it's not just in our major cities that recess has become a casualty of testing. FairTest cites numerous examples of recess lost and nap time gone missing. Here's just one troubling example:

> In Kenosha, Wisconsin, parents were shocked when the principal of the Bain School of Arts and Language announced that recess would be eliminated because the school's test scores threatened to place it on the state's watch list of schools not meeting NCLB test score standards. "If teachers want to bring their students outside, it will be only for educational purposes and will include studying," said Bain Principal Margaret Carpenter.[6]

If the only reason our children are given a break from their studies is so that they can study some more, we fear we might already have fallen down a rabbit hole.

DUMBING DOWN WHAT'S LEFT

Tests drive instruction. They will continue to do so as long as anyone cares about the scores, and merely publishing the results for each community school in the local newspaper is enough to give the scores weight and cause people to worry about them. So we need to stay alert to the direction in which the tests are driving instruction. We think it is clear that the current frenzy of accountability testing is driving instruction *away from* complex, long-term projects and investigations whose outcomes aren't known and whose evaluation depends to some extent on direct human judgment. The outsized emphasis on test scores has driven instruction toward items with one clear, right answer, in an attempt to prepare students for what really counts—the standardized test.

You'll often hear someone say that a good test is one that teachers should be pleased to teach to. But this proposition concerns us. When it comes to whether teaching to the test is a worthy goal, we don't worry so much about the items on the test. (That's a matter we touched on to some extent in chapter 1 and will examine again in chapter 8.) If we don't overinterpret what the tests are capable of telling us, we shouldn't do too much damage. However, we think that a far more important issue is almost always overlooked in policy discussions: *what's not on the test.*

Of course, whole subject areas that aren't tested won't be on the test. But even in those subjects that are tested—primarily ELA and math and to a lesser extent science—many important outcomes are just too complex for the kind of assessments we're willing to pay for. So whether a high school algebra student really understands functions is not going to be clear from one or two multiple-choice items. Surely eight or ten individual items would do a better job, but what would be far more revealing would be to hear the student explain the "vertical line" test and offer some thoughts on why the whole question of functions matters. But you won't get this kind of depth from a standardized test with multiple-choice or even short-answer items. And even worse, you won't get this kind of learning if you teach to such a test.

There is a push-and-pull, give-and-take kind of relationship between what goes on in classrooms and the assessments we use to monitor that activity. What we think we know about schooling leads us to pursue different kinds of assessments, just as what we think we know about assessments influences what and how we teach. And recent history bears this out. When the notion was afoot in the land that schools were graduating vast armies of utter illiterates (never true), we sought tests that would "guarantee" minimum competency.[7] This period was roughly from the late 1960s to the early 1980s. After that, the response to the 1983 report *A Nation at Risk* pushed minimum competency testing into the background and replaced it with the test-driven pursuit of high standards.

Those minimum-competency tests didn't ask a great deal of the students who took them. Indeed, they weren't meant to. Partly in response to the low level of these tests, the idea gained currency that important learning depended on unique situations and could be judged only in a real context. Consequently, a movement toward authentic assessment (judging students on a task and in a setting as close to its real-world counterpart as possible) or the more narrowly focused performance assessment (e.g., assessing the completion of a scientific experiment) was born.[8] While this movement remains active, it is largely off the radar screen of discussions of national assessment policy. The movement began in the late 1970s and had its heyday in the early 1990s.

The outcomes of many kinds of assessments in context proved difficult to quantify, and that made it hard to use performance assessments or most other forms of authentic assessment to judge schools and educators. In response, new voices called for both higher standards and for holding schools and educators accountable in some quantifiable way for seeing that students meet the standards. This standards movement began in the very early 1990s, waned in the later 1990s, but has picked up steam again in recent years with the new focus on what are called the Common Core Standards now being hawked by the Obama administration and other policy heavy hitters.[9] It has contributed greatly to creating the current tsunami of high-stakes standardized testing that we have been experiencing for more than a decade. It remains the dominant view of accountability. We have contended throughout this book that this view—especially in its focus on holding someone accountable for test scores—distorts the efforts of educators to provide nuanced and engaging learning experiences for their students.

For some time, thoughtful educators have been wary of the danger that a chosen approach to measurement will have too much impact on what is to be measured, that the test will drive instruction whether we want it to or not. How long have they been worried? Try at least a century, give or take a generation. Sharon Nichols and David Berliner cite a report from the New York State Department of Education:

- It is a great and more serious evil, by too frequent and too numerous examinations, so to magnify their importance that students come to regard them not as a means in education but as the final purpose, the ultimate goal.
- It is a very great and more serious evil to sacrifice systematic instruction and a comprehensive view of the subject for the scrappy and unrelated knowledge gained by students who are persistently drilled in the mere answering of questions issued by the Education Department or other governing bodies.[10]

The language of this report no doubt tipped you off that it isn't referring to NCLB or to the new Obama "blueprint"—or anything else in living memory. It was issued in 1906, long before the modern psychometric industry was born. Certainly the tests would have been different in those days. But how different? To illustrate, here are a few items taken from the 1913 Winter Term Examinations used in Michigan, which are no doubt similar to those referred to by the New York State Department:

Second Grade: Arithmetic

1) Mention five things that are sold by the pint, quart, and gallon.
2) Mention three things that are sold by the bushel.
3) How many quarts are there in a bushel? In a gallon? In a half bushel?
4) How many are two 2's? Four 5's? Eight 3's? Three 8's?
5) If a boy can run from first base to second in 12 seconds, in how long a time can he make a home run at the same rate?[11]

Certainly, these weren't machine-scored, multiple-choice exams, but they still show that the problems of item writing were around a hundred years ago. Take that boy running from first to second base in twelve seconds, for example. He's either a very young boy, a preschooler perhaps, or he's pulling his little brother in a wagon. In either case, we don't think he's going to be called safe. Trying to place test items with simple answers in a facsimile of the real world was then—and remains today—a tough task. What's more, while in the early twentieth century it might have been useful to know what commodities were sold by the bushel, even then it hardly constituted a measure of comprehensive thinking or higher-order skills. Our point in listing these items here is that, once we get past the quaintness of the content that might have been important in 1913, the complaint from the New York Department of Education remains apt: There is a risk of focusing on the test results rather than on the learning. The warning to be careful to keep the scrappy test from leading to an equally scrappy education amounts to a kind of "prequantitative" version of Campbell's Law.

But before we pass on from these early standardized tests—and they were standardized in that all teachers were given directions so that they could administer them in the same way—we want to share an example of a very sophisticated question from those Michigan exams that doesn't lend itself well to the current methods of multiple-choice or even fill-in-the-blanks kinds of standardized tests.

Fourth-graders in Michigan were asked as part of their geography tests (today, the question would fall under the heading of science) to "explain the changes of the moon." "Explaining" is really hard to do when you're blackening in a bubble with a No. 2 pencil, and it's even harder to measure in any quantitative way. But before you chuckle at how naive our great-great-grandparents were to have asked such a simple question, don't dismiss the complexity of what it's trying to find out. Try answering it. You can even wave your hands if that helps, as it sometimes does. If you're a teacher, ask your students; if you're a parent, ask your children—fourth-graders and up— and see what they come up with.

So you don't think that this is just a silly exercise, remember that it assumes you know something about the relative locations of the sun, the earth, and the moon and that you know about how the moon revolves around the earth and rotates on its axis. Moreover, you don't need to know anything about the earth's shadow. The phases of the moon are not part of a slow-motion, month-long eclipse. Even today's university students seem to need some help, and we recommend a refresher in the form of a really instructive interactive website for Astronomy 103 at http://brahms.phy.vanderbilt. edu/a103/labs/web_moonphases.shtml. Whether or not you are a classroom teacher, if you're not quite secure in your own understanding of "the changes of the moon," you will want to visit the site before you talk with your kids.

The phases of the moon ought to be something we can assume everyone understands, especially since our species has now visited the moon several times and has plans to return. But in a world where high school graduation, being promoted to the next grade, and even a teacher's salary can depend on scores on standardized tests, what becomes of such important knowledge? As a result of our obsessive focus on test scores, it becomes one more example of what's missing from today's curriculum.

Teaching students about something as visible to everyone on the planet as the phases of the moon shouldn't be left to chance or even the Discovery Channel. Yet real understanding of this phenomenon tends to fall by the wayside in favor of what can be asked on one of the high-stakes tests that currently drive the curriculum in many of our schools. But like creativity and cooperation, like learning to recognize and solve problems that aren't trivial, like learning the skills of design or the skills of negotiation, indeed, like dozens of other important kinds of knowledge and skill, understanding the phases of the moon is pushed aside. If there's time on a Friday afternoon for a little science lesson on the solar system, great. If not, well, we have to prepare for the next round of tests, and we know that they will consist mostly of the twenty-first-century equivalent of "mention three things that are sold by the bushel."As an aside in this chapter, we alluded to more authentic ways to assess student performance. In chapter 8, we'll examine some of the reasons why we don't routinely judge students' learning by means of such more authentic measures, whether alone or in conjunction with more familiar paper-and-pencil tests.

Ⓐ Ⓑ Ⓒ Ⓓ

KIDS OR COWS? TOM O'BRIEN

What use of standardized tests would I recommend? Not much. Their limited vision presents a number of obstacles.

For openers, testing is invoked to give a sort of automatic blessing to a policy or practice because it is "research-based." In large-scale paper-and-pencil testing involving, say, algebra courses, we might well wonder which of the many possible "algebras" was tested. How does the test match what was taught in children's classrooms? What attention did the test give to such lightweight stuff as rules and vocabulary? What attention was given to students' higher-order thinking and the structure of the knowledge? What is the effect of such tests on what happens in the classroom? That is, has algebra in classrooms become one with the test? Educators need to read the research reported and understand what it means for their teaching and their students' learning.

Standardized tests can quickly classify large numbers of subjects into categories. For example, in medicine it is helpful to know which groups of people are likely to be most susceptible to a virus so that precautions can be taken on their behalf. This makes sense. And it makes sense to cull cattle according to certain criteria so that a malady such as "mad cow" disease can be kept in check. In educational situations, things are usually far more complex.

One global aspect of standardized testing is that it usually treats students as passive. It asks, What is the effect of the curriculum on the student? More sensible and more productive is to turn the question around: What is the effect of the organism on the treatment? Or in educational terms: What does the child make of the things that are taught? Kids are, if anything, active. The treatment acts on them, but they act on the treatment as well. What are the relationships, uses, ideas, and extensions that the kids construct? Kids are not mere memory storage bins to be sorted according to the number of correct answers they hold. A simple real-life situation makes the point.

A colleague and I once asked five-year-old Bobby, "What is 9 plus 9?" He replied confidently, "19."

What now? Instead of judging the answer incorrect, as a test-scoring device would, we explored further.

"How come?"

"Well, 10 and 10 is 20. And 9 is 1 less than 10."

"So?"

"So 9 plus 9 is 19."

With some insight into Bobby's thinking, we next asked, "What's 9 plus 10?"

"Oh, that's 19. That other thing we started with, 9 + 9, that's 18!"

What would have happened if no follow-up was made after the child answered 19? Bang, like a cow carrying "mad cow" disease, he'd be sorted from the herd into the class of low-achievers, perhaps never to return. But what you see here is a child thinking, not merely filling in a bubble. And the quality of the child's thinking is exceptionally complex for a five-year-old. Bobby's response was relational, not static, and so it can lead to the construction of new knowledge.

It seems to me that the very purpose of education is to provide nutrition for children's minds and emotions. Assessment should provide information for teachers to make decisions that nourish kids. Bubble sheets with pencil marks show the aftermath of a child's processing. They do not provide nutrition. Most commonly, they lead us only to cull the herd.

Tom O'Brien, a former NATO senior research fellow in science, is an educator and researcher who is interested in how children achieve understanding.

8

Why Not More Direct Measurement?

Standardized tests that assess only low-level skills and that can be scored electronically cost very little to administer, although their hidden costs are enormous. . . .

—Richard Rothstein, Rebecca Jacobsen, and Tamara Wilder, 2009

When teens are approaching the legal age to operate a motor vehicle, it's not unusual to see them with a copy of their state's driver's manual protruding from some pocket or other. Having the manual close at hand enables them to study—anywhere, any time—the rules of the road that they will need to know when they take the written exam for a driver's license. For example, they'll need to know road signs and be able to identify them from the outlines alone. But it's a no-brainer that knowing the rules of the road and acing the written test don't make someone a safe driver.

To find out whether or not that's true, there's the road test, the kind of direct measurement of the skill to be assessed that we allude to in the title of this chapter. The basic assumption that we wish to examine in this chapter grows out of our indiscriminate use of standardized testing: *An indirect measure of knowledge or skill (the test) is better than a direct measure (the actual performance).*

In a lot of ways, the road test for a driver's license is the model of a direct measure of an important skill. Certainly, it's a test of performance in the real world. How hard should I apply the brakes? Is there time to enter this roadway safely? Is the sky overcast enough to require headlights? But like any performance test, this one is built on a foundation of knowledge. In the case of the driver's test, it's the information contained in the driver's manual.

Before you decide how forcefully to apply the brakes, you need to recognize the stop sign and know what it means. And if you want full credit from your examiner, you'll also need to bring your car to rest behind the white line for the crosswalk.

But even the road test isn't always the end of the probationary period for new drivers. In many states, further restrictions apply to drivers under a certain age until they've logged enough time—usually three or six months—as licensed drivers. Sometimes, for example, new drivers aren't allowed to drive after a certain time of day, unless the trip is to or from work or school. In a way, this practice recognizes that performance tests such as the road test are also samples of the broad suite of behaviors we expect every driver to have mastered. The state examiner selects a sample of important behaviors to examine on the day the student earns his or her license. But the additional probationary period is intended to allow the state to sample an even broader range of important behaviors before awarding full driving privileges. Unlike assessing student performance in school, we are not satisfied with judgments rendered on a narrow sample of behavior. Presumably, we can all drive a little more confidently as a result.

If this system of combining a performance assessment with a paper-and-pencil test is such a good one, why don't we use it for all our testing needs? That's a good question, with a complicated answer. Before we delve into that, though, we want to put before you a premise we take to be basic to all assessment. That really sounds portentous, doesn't it? But our premise is simple: The more important the knowledge or skill we want to measure, the closer we should try to come to the actual performance itself.

Take heart surgery, for example. Say you're in the unenviable position of having to choose a doctor for a coronary bypass. Certainly, high grades in college, good MCAT (medical college admission test) scores, and good grades in first-year science courses in medical school will serve as measures of what your doctor knows. (In chapter 9, we'll get to see how good some of those measures are—or are not—at predicting your doctor's performance.) And surely what a doctor knows is related to his or her success rate. But added to all these indirect measures, we would also be more than a little curious to know how many similar surgeries our potential doctor has performed. Or for a newer physician, how many procedures has he or she assisted? These are more direct measures of the particular skill we're interested in knowing about, and we think you'll agree that they provide an important kind of information that we can use to make such an important decision.

Where educational assessment is concerned, we don't seem to try very hard to find a direct measure of actual performance. When it comes to judging our

schools, teachers, and students, we accept standardized test scores as definitive measures of performance. As we've argued throughout this book, these
tests aren't nearly as good as most people believe them to be even at assessing
basic knowledge and skills. For assessing the broad array of outcomes that
we want from our schools, they are even less useful. In chapters 10 and 11,
we'll take up the goals and purposes of schools and introduce you to some
new thinking about what a useful accountability system might look like. But
for now, we believe everyone can agree that those goals and purposes are
much broader than simple skills in reading and math. And for public services
(clearly including education), "quantitative measures of performance [are]
mostly inappropriate" because they have "goals that can't easily be defined
in simple numerical terms."[1]

Why then do we settle for standardized test scores—indirect measures of
school outcomes—when they aren't even all that good at what they're designed to measure? Why do we press these indirect measures into service as
faulty gauges of the health of our education system? We believe there are two
reasons. First, we all know that the cost of most kinds of direct measurement
will be much higher. And that means higher taxes, and no one wants that.
However, we also believe that there is a second reason, a kind of bureaucratic
inertia that simply accepts and builds on past practices, even when those
practices, when closely examined, seem obviously silly. We begin there and
work our way back to cost.

BUREAUCRATIC INERTIA

Let us share a follow-up to the tale of the tests in "Bruce's Story" (page
65). This little coda is a good illustration of what we mean by bureaucratic
inertia.

When he first learned that he would need to take the Graduate Record Examination (GRE) in order to apply to doctoral programs, Bruce read up on it.
Its ostensible purpose—then and now—was to judge whether or not someone
would be able to succeed in graduate school. But he had already been successful in graduate school, had acquired a master's degree, and had written a
thesis on the travel books of Graham Greene. Any doctoral program would
have enough information in the form of transcripts, grades, written work, and
recommendations to judge whether he would be a valuable addition to its
stable of graduate teaching assistants. Once he pointed out these obvious facts
to the admissions committees, Bruce reasoned, all would be well. Surely, he
could forget about the GRE, no?

No! When the doctoral programs received his application, they noted the absence of GRE scores and insisted on having them, and soon. "What's the point?" he argued. "Doesn't success in graduate school, which the test tries to predict, mean more than a score that's just a stand-in for that real-world experience?" But even the university that had awarded his master's degree said it needed his GRE scores to process his application.

A light began to dawn. Although we say we accept the weak predictions of future success that test scores provide because they are the *best evidence we have* of a target behavior, that's not actually true. Look at the tests we use as part of our higher education admission system.

The SAT is intended to predict first-year college grades, though even for that purpose it is a mediocre predictor and not quite as good by itself as high school grades alone. Together, grades and SAT scores are only slightly better at predicting first-year college grades than either is alone. But the difference is just a few percentage points.[2] So the SAT is certainly *not* the best measure we have available to forecast students' first-year college grades—assuming that first-year grades are something we even care that much about.

There is more dispute about the predictive power of the GRE for a couple of reasons. First, the pool of would-be graduate students who take the GRE is highly diverse in subject area because the students have already specialized as undergrads; second, the range of the test takers is highly restricted because most people going on to grad school are among the higher achievers, those who flourished in an academic setting.[3] But whether the correlation with future academic or career success is strong or weak or mediocre seems moot if the actual behavior in question—success in graduate school—is available and can be documented. Why would anyone still need to examine a less-than-stellar predictor? Clearly, we're dealing with bureaucratic inertia: The rules say we have to have the scores, so we have to have them. And since we have to have them, we suppose we ought to pay some attention to them. So we do.

So Bruce took the GRE, got great scores, and began to rethink the relationship of assessment to the entire enterprise of schooling. It boils down to a matter of using the best tool for the job. If a standardized test is the best tool available, then by all means, let's use it—whether it's the SAT, the GRE, or whatever test your state uses to judge how well its schools are doing. But if you've been following us through the preceding chapters, we think you'll agree that, generally speaking, this is not how we do things. Instead of opting for the best tool available, we pick up whatever tool is handy, provided the cost is low enough, and apply it to whatever job we're trying to do. And this leads to some absurd consequences.

Looking back, what can we make of the panic—not too strong a word—kindled by the math portion of the GRE in the hearts of many of Bruce's

English Department peers? These young English majors were bright, had read widely, and were highly articulate. Some were quite adept at math, of course, but others hadn't studied any math since high school, as much as a decade in the past, and then only enough to be admitted to college.

So why the requirement? And why for everyone? Well, we had this math test already developed, see, and we have a math and verbal section on the SAT, see. So we thought we'd just use it to rank potential graduate students in all fields. The smart ones know this stuff anyway, don't they?

Maybe not. The future performance of students of English and American literature has precious little to do with their understanding and recall of high school mathematics. And its title notwithstanding, the *Graduate* Record Examination assesses mostly shopkeeper math, a little algebra and geometry, and not much beyond. For those pursuing graduate degrees in math, science, or engineering—and for refugees from these fields, like Bruce—it's a snap, and the test provides little useful information to the programs they are applying to. But for most of those who study classical languages? or English? or art history? What does the test say about them? The quantitative portion of the GRE simply doesn't tell us *anything useful* about the graduate school performance of these budding scholars. The test is just one more hoop to jump through—and a particularly meaningless one at that. It seems to be an exercise in absurdity. Something else must be going on.

And that something is simply this: Our national infatuation with testing has caused us to confuse means and ends. If the test is a stand-in—however good or bad—for future performance, a demonstration of that actual performance is by definition better and ought to make the stand-in unnecessary. But the means (the test) have become more important than the end (finding a good match between students and graduate programs). In some ways, this confusion of means and ends is a lot like the distortions that Campbell's Law predicts when high stakes are attached to quantitative indicators. Our attention becomes riveted on the wrong things.

Why, then, don't we seek out more direct measures of students' success in school or college? Many people will argue that these more direct measures are "not as reliable as standardized tests." That is, if you examined the same skill directly in context for a second time, you would be less likely to get the same outcome than you would be if you used a standardized test for the examination. Fair enough. Those standardized tests were designed to be at least somewhat reliable. But we can't let reliability trump validity—or common sense. If you give a Shakespearean scholar a math test today, and he fails miserably because he has avoided math since junior year in high school, he is very likely to fail a similar test tomorrow. So the test has great reliability! But it has no validity. That is, it tells you precisely nothing about what you want to know: the Shakespearean's aptitude for graduate study in Elizabethan literature. This is the kind of absurdity that is always created when means are confused with ends.

COST VERSUS VALUE

Others who argue for indirect measures like standardized tests in place of more direct measures will cite the cost of the latter. And they are certainly right that assessing students' knowledge directly will be expensive in terms of time and personnel. Having someone sit down with a student to work through a one-on-one assessment of the student's reading ability is indeed costly. Individual attention of this kind is one reason that special education, with its required Individualized Education Program (IEP), is so much costlier per student than mainstream education. Or consider the relative cost of scoring a multiple-choice item as opposed to an essay item. "It costs 50 cents to $5 to score an essay, compared with pennies for each multiple-choice question."[4] That's a pretty wide range of costs for the essay scoring, but depending on length and complexity, it seems sensible. Meanwhile, an entire multiple-choice exam can be bought, administered, and scored for about the same price as one fairly complex essay item.[5]

But we think it's important to keep in mind, however, that cost and value are not the same. Richard Rothstein, Rebecca Jacobsen, and Tamara Wilder have pointed out that "standardized tests that assess only low-level skills and that can be scored electronically cost very little to administer, although their hidden costs are enormous in the lost opportunities to develop young people's broader knowledge, traits, and skills."[6] Exactly. And those hidden opportunity costs—what we don't do because it's not tested—suggest that we need to be judicious in deciding what to assess, how often, and at what level.

The worth of any assessment depends on whether it generates information that is useful in helping people make inferences about performance in a particular domain. Does the assessment help you answer important questions? Trying to get closer to actual performance in a particular domain might be more expensive in terms of dollars, but it requires less interpretation of what the outcomes mean. For example, would it be useful to know that a prospective graduate student in medieval literature had presented a paper on *Beowulf* at a national conference? Seems probable. It's certainly a measure of that student's talent and commitment to the field. What about how well or in how many ways that student could solve a system of three simultaneous linear equations? Not so much.

It's not all that hard to sort this out. We just need to keep our focus on *what we want to learn* through our assessments, *why* we want to learn it, and *how much* we're prepared to spend to be right. As in the last several chapters, we've not directly criticized the standardized tests and the technologies that support them in this chapter. Instead, we've questioned the misguided ways we use them.

In chapter 9, we'll look at just how good our standardized tests are at answering questions about the future, and in the final two chapters, we'll say some things about how we think we should go about deciding why, what, and how to assess. For now, the takeaway message of this chapter is that some of our current requirements with regard to testing simply don't make sense.

THE TESTS WE NEED TODAY, GAIL MARSHALL

Historically, the development and use of standardized tests has evolved in form and function to meet a specific need. For example, British and American civil service exams were tailored to the perceived needs of the departments involved; the Army Alpha Test was designed to screen into the service men who could read; the SAT was originally designed to select students who would be able to carry on their courses of study in college. Today's state accountability tests are designed to tell "how much" students have learned. They are not designed to say "how" children learn, which must be the question asked if the test results are to be used to help children learn. But there are tests that can provide clues as to the types of errors in thinking kids make.

Moreover, today's accountability-type tests are designed for a pretech era, when finding out how well kids recall information might have made more sense. Today, we need a population that does more than store data. We need a population that can *act on* data, *make sense* of data, and *use* data in novel ways. Today's state tests are modeled on the old SAT and either tap into "stored knowledge" directly or tap into stored knowledge to be acted upon by formulae kids should know. What we really want in 2011 and beyond is to know that students are capable of complex learning and acting.

An example of an item that can help us understand how kids think might clarify things. Consider the analogy "King is to ? as count is to countess." Because "queen" is the most frequently occurring word association response to "king," children who give this answer could simply be working on the basis of a word association and not acting on the underlying logical relation. But try this analogy: "King is to ? as beggar is to rags." Now, the correct response is not *queen* but *robes*. If you look at the data in response to such an item, you can see a relation between correct responses and achievement test scores: the children who choose robes are usually high achievers in other areas. From that we deduce that they can suppress the immediate word association response and make a logical analysis.

We need tests that show children acting on information (thinking) and suppressing immediate associations (reacting). But today's test developers are seldom folks who have a deep knowledge of children's ways of thinking. They are "item bank technicians."

Gail Marshall holds a PhD in cognitive psychology and psychometrics. She has designed prize-winning software for Sunburst Communications and has contributed articles to numerous educational technology journals.

9

The Tests Don't Predict Well

The best predictors of future high-level, real-life accomplishment in writing, science, art, music, and leadership are similar accomplishments.

—Leonard Baird, 1985

Way back in 1921, Lewis Terman, who might well be dubbed the father of IQ testing in America, decided to study child geniuses. He and his colleagues at Stanford University chose 1,521 children whose IQ scores were at least 140, placing them in the top 1 percent of the population.[1] But Terman and his colleagues did more than just study these children with exceptionally high IQs; they continued to follow them throughout their lives, making for one of the longest longitudinal studies of individuals on record.

Here are a few intriguing items gathered over all those years of tracking a group whose members cheerfully embraced the name they were popularly know by: Terman's Termites.

- William Shockley, coinventor of the transistor and 1956 Nobel Laureate in physics, didn't make the cut because his IQ score wasn't high enough.
- Luis Alvarez, 1968 Nobelist in physics for elementary particle research, also didn't make the cut.
- None of the Termites has been awarded a Nobel Prize in any field.
- But the Termites didn't do so badly either: Three became members of the National Academy of Sciences, eighty-one (including twelve women) were listed in "American Men of Science," and collectively they have registered 350 patents. Next time President Obama delivers a stem-winder oration, you can thank Termite Jess Oppenheimer, inventor of the TelePrompTer. [2]

So what does it all mean? We promised in the Introduction that we wouldn't be jumping into the swamp of controversy that has surrounded IQ testing since its origin, and we're holding to that. Biologists are finally getting past most of their nature-versus-nurture hang-ups as they learn more and more about the intimate connections of all facets of genetics and the environment. But in the social sciences, especially where IQ is concerned, the battle has raged for nearly a century, with the hereditarians going to war with the environmentalists in nearly every decade of the twentieth century. For a good introduction to that history, along with what we judge to be a strong antihereditarian argument (close to our own position), we recommend *The Mismeasure of Man*, by Stephen Jay Gould.

In this chapter, though, we're willing to dip our toes briefly into at least part of that mess as we try to see what and how well standardized tests of any kind can make predictions. Terman, who gave the world the term *IQ*, published the Stanford Revision of the intelligence scales used in France by Alfred Binet and Theodore Simon. Still, though he created the new version of the IQ test, Terman thought it was important to see how well his creation matched up against the subsequent life experiences of those he tested. And he was particularly interested in how well the test measured the abilities of those with scores at the highest levels. In other words, Terman was not prepared to accept untested the basic assumption about standardized testing that we're addressing in this chapter: *Standardized tests are the best predictors of future success in school and in life.*

WHAT DO WE KNOW?

Where to begin? We know that scores on standardized tests—whether IQ tests, school achievement tests, or college and graduate school admission tests—predict performance on other standardized tests. That's a function of the way they're all created. For example, standard IQ tests correlate somewhere between 0.70 and 0.85 with such "achievement" tests as the Iowa Tests of Basic Skills.[3] Recall that correlation is simply a measure of the association between two variables, in this case scores on two different tests. As a rule of thumb, a correlation between two variables that falls between 0.60 and 0.80 is generally said to be substantial, and those higher than 0.80 are considered very high indeed. Going a step further, though, when we want to say how much of the difference in one variable is associated with difference in the other variable, we need to square the correlation. So 0.80 becomes 0.64, and we say that one variable "explains" or "accounts for" (still doesn't mean causes) 64 percent of the variance in the other. The high correlations between differing kinds of standardized tests strongly suggest that they are half-siblings at least.

The curious thing about the tests used for school accountability and college admission is that there have been so few studies—especially recent ones—of the relationship between test scores and future success, especially success outside the classroom. The most comprehensive and important such study was a review of the literature by Leonard Baird.[4] Baird's study, though, was published in 1985 and nothing even remotely as comprehensive has appeared in the decades since—this despite the increasing emphasis on testing in our education system. But Baird didn't just examine test scores and later success; he also looked at studies of the connection between grades and later success. We'll say a bit about what Baird found—and didn't find—below. But the dearth of studies itself raises a few questions.

Let us first try to say why there just aren't studies of the connection between the tests used for accountability and later success. It's not that we don't want to know whether these tests can be linked to important outcomes later in life. Those who don't like the tests would be cheered to find solid evidence that they don't say anything about the future, while those who do like them would be cheered to learn that they predict important outcomes.

But such studies would be next to impossible to do. To track the connection between a ten-year-old's scores on a state accountability exam and that child's subsequent success in life would mean tracking individual children for a minimum of twenty years. Before computers and digitally archived data, this was a completely unthinkable prospect in a mobile society like the United States. Even with vastly improved data collection and storage, the cost remains prohibitive, so we don't make the attempt. (The same impediments also explain why we can't arrive at anything like a solid figure for the dropout rate: It has simply been too costly to track individual students as they move around and in and out of schools.)

So the research Baird analyzed looked primarily at such measures as admissions tests for colleges and graduate and professional schools (SAT, ACT, GRE, LSAT, etc.), some tests of creativity, and such things as high school grades and accomplishments both inside and outside of schools (working on the yearbook, creating art, playing sports, organizing student groups, etc.). What he found overall he described as "low positive relationships between academic aptitude and/or grades and accomplishment."[5]

As we searched for information in this area, we canvassed a number of our professional connections. One noted research analyst whom we consulted put it this way:

A conspiracy theorist might wonder why there seems to be nothing after Baird's report. . . . I think it might be that the College Board's report on the SAT decline, and especially *A Nation at Risk*, cemented the myth that test scores were essential to getting good jobs, coupled with the rising belief that jobs are what education is all about.[6]

Even in 1985, Baird recognized that, before we worried very much about the size of the connection between tests or grades and future performance, we needed to be able to answer a simple two-part question: "Why should we expect to find a relationship between academic ability and/or grades and real-life accomplishment?" and "Why should we expect to find *little* relationship between academic ability and real-life accomplishment?" To the first question, Baird was pretty much reduced to answering, "Because we believe it's true." Here's how he put it:

More often than not the answers or logic are presumed and not spelled out. Perhaps the most basic assumption is that academic ability plays a large or at least contributing role in success in most human activities. The ordinary person might express this as "you've got to be smart to do a really good job or to get ahead"— with "smart" usually meaning that a person would do well in school or would have skills that would lead him or her to score high on a test of academic ability.[7]

When Baird uses the phrase *academic ability*, he's usually referring to test scores of some kind. For grades and accomplishments, he generally says grades and accomplishments. We don't intend to question his motives by pointing this out. There's no deception involved. Rather, we think it reflects just what Baird is saying about the "presumed logic" of the testing situation. We teach knowledge and skills in our nation's classrooms that we *believe* are important to adult life. The grades teachers give students are measures of how well students learn the knowledge and skills we offer them, but grades also reflect many other things—among them perseverance, motivation, creativity, the ability to cooperate, and so on. Grades will always reflect this broader range. Tests clearly aim to measure knowledge and skills alone, and not other attributes, so we might suppose that test scores would more clearly reveal any connection between school learning and life success. (How well tests succeed in measuring knowledge and skills is also a matter of some debate, as our earlier chapters have pointed out.)

Baird's answer to the second question—Why should we expect to find *little* relationship between academic ability and real-life accomplishment?— focuses on technical issues and involves less hand-waving. One primary reason he cites is the diversity of human activity. Baird argues that it "seems unreasonable" to believe that scientific research, office management, political leadership, community service, religious leadership, journalism, and so on could all be highly related to the same measures of academic ability. (We might have written the same words.) Moreover, he points out how activities that are seemingly similar can be very situation specific. Think, for example, of John Sculley's unsuccessful efforts to bring his success as CEO of Pepsico to Apple Computer. Both companies faced competitors who dominated the field. Sculley succeeded at Pepsi, but it took the return of Steve Jobs to the top post at Apple to bring the company out of the doldrums.

Baird's list of technical reasons why we shouldn't expect to find a connection between academic ability, as measured by tests or grades, and subsequent success is lengthy. He cites difficulties defining "success" or accomplishment. Salary, for example, is clearly a false indicator for many careers, including teaching and other service professions. He mentions the length of time between the assessment of academic ability (test or classroom grade) and the life accomplishment; much can happen in a couple of decades that would obscure any relationship that might once have existed. He also cites the problem of the "restricted range" of abilities. For example, most doctors have high grades and test scores or they wouldn't have gotten into medical school, so merely by being admitted to study for the profession, they've been preselected for academic ability and achievement on several occasions.

When you read Baird's speculations about the likelihood of finding connections between grades and test scores and subsequent life success, you no longer wonder why there have been so few studies in this area. Indeed, you might ask why Baird himself persisted, but we're glad he did. Even negative or weak connections can lead to insight. And weak is the appropriate way to characterize what Baird found.

Before we leave our explicit look at Baird's study, we think one of the most interesting things he found was that the connection between "nonacademic accomplishment" (e.g., organizing a student group, publishing a poem, exhibiting one's artwork, taking part in a National Science Foundation summer workshop) and later accomplishment both in college and in life was stronger than the connection between grades or test scores and later accomplishment. Baird examined so many studies that it's impossible to summarize all the data he presented; he spent more than eighty pages doing so. But in one of the larger studies he examined, the correlations between test scores and grades and subsequent accomplishments in specific areas ranged from -0.08 to +0.27. The strongest *median* correlations he found were for GPA and "leadership" (at +0.15, explaining about 2 percent of the variance) and for test scores and "science" accomplishments (at +0.09, explaining less than 1 percent). Weak indeed. And Baird seems to agree. For admissions committees that wish to select outstanding students who will eventually contribute the most to society, he recommends looking carefully at "noninstitution sponsored" accomplishments:

> [T]he most efficient information for predicting future accomplishments is data on previous accomplishments. The studies reviewed here show that the best predictors of future high-level, real-life accomplishment in writing, science, art, music, and leadership are similar accomplishments, albeit at a lower level, in previous years. . . . [T]he most effective predictor of high-level accomplishment is past high-level behaviors of the same or similar types.[8]

The accomplishments we want to predict do not include scores on future tests. As Gerald Bracey put it in his latest book, "Once people leave educational institutions, they don't usually have to take any test that looks like what they suffered through in high school."[9] Of course, they do organize things, manage things, cooperate with co-workers, generate solutions to new and ill-defined problems, and so on.

A COUNTERVAILING VIEW

Overall, most studies that try to predict future performance are a kind of faith-based exercise. We say that because, while grades usually do a better job of predicting performance than test scores, neither is a slam dunk for its proponents. Baird's study showed this much clearly. Yet the results of these "predictive" studies are often touted as more far-reaching than they could possibly be—and more general than the actual studies claim. As an example, take a recent volley fired from the tests-are-better-predictors-than-grades side.

In 2007, *Science*, the weekly flagship publication of the American Association for the Advancement of Science (AAAS), published in its Education Forum a report of a study that ran under the headline "Standardized Tests Predict Graduate Student Success."[10] Well, yes and no. The authors of the study are strong proponents of the predictive validity of test scores. They make no secret of the fact. Indeed, they are strong proponents of the "*g* factor," the general factor often equated with general intelligence, first identified—not to say invented—by Charles Spearman and much beloved by Lewis Terman and others.

But the claim in the headline is a bit overstated. The strongest predictions cited are for the scores on the Medical College Admissions Test (MCAT) and success in subsequent licensing exams (remember, tests usually predict other tests pretty well); for scores on the GRE and success in doctoral qualifying exams (ditto); and for scores on the MCAT and first-year grade-point average in medical school. While the connections between tests and other tests come as no surprise, it might seem surprising that first-year medical school GPA would be predicted better by the MCAT (a correlation of about 0.60, a pretty fair correlation that accounts for about 36 percent of the difference) than by undergraduate grades. But on reflection it's not all that stunning. The first year of medical school is essentially a fifth year of biological and medical science classes—biochemistry, genetics, anatomy, physiology, embryology, etc. It makes intuitive sense that tests like the MCAT, which cover a highly specific domain, will be fairly good—despite all their flaws—at forecasting the grades students will earn in specifically academic courses in the medical sciences. So while the information is interesting, and the study appears to be sound, we're not altogether surprised.

But not everyone was so accepting of the study and its findings when it appeared. Bob Schaeffer, education director of FairTest, dubbed it "a meta-analysis of pro-testing meta-analyses," and he further likened the study to research sponsored by the tobacco industry to demonstrate that cigarettes do not cause cancer.[11] That's a pretty harsh charge to level against anyone these days. While the authors do have connections to the testing industry, the lead author, Nathan Kuncel, maintains that no industry funds supported the research and that only one of the studies in their dataset was supported by the testing industry. We take him at his word.

You would be within your rights, though, to ask if we are not guilty of trying to undercut the impact of this study because we just don't like its conclusions. Well, that may be partly true, because we don't much care for them. But just as the authors of the study reject the accusation that they were straining to find studies that support tests over grades, so we maintain that we are trying to be fair to them. We surely don't intend to impugn their motives. However, the one thing we find somewhat surprising in their results is that even ETS, which owns and operates the GRE, hasn't historically made such large claims for its predictive power. Earlier ETS materials have claimed correlations of about 0.33 between first-year grades in grad school and GRE scores. The authors of the current study corrected for the "restricted range" of grad school applicants. That is, because they're all successful undergrads, there won't be much of a range of difference for the tests to predict. They also took account of the small range of grad school grades; they're almost all A's and B's—and that's not grade inflation, for it has long been that way, and in many graduate programs a grade of C carries no credit toward a degree. We just wonder why ETS didn't make the corrections that Kuncel and coauthor Sarah Hezlett did in order to use the higher correlations in the company's own promotional materials.

In any case, ETS was less than satisfied with the success of the GRE and in 2006 announced major changes. By 2007, though, ETS had decided instead to make only a series of minor changes over time. The most prominent of these changes is the addition of some "fill in the blanks" items. But in response to demands from deans and other leaders of higher education, in 2009 ETS began offering a Personal Potential Index (PPI), an evaluation of such personal attributes as "Knowledge and Creativity; Communication Skills; Teamwork; Resilience; Planning and Organization; and Ethics and Integrity."[12] While the new PPI is optional, it is included at no additional charge as part of the $140 fee paid by GRE takers.

Finally, the authors of the *Science* study conclude, as did Baird and as the admissions test makers have been advising since the tests came into widespread use in the decades after World War II, that because tests improve the predictions made by grades alone, the two measures should be used together to select incoming classes. This is true as far as it goes. But the questions we ask in the next section are: How much improvement? and At what cost?[13]

TAKEN AS DIRECTED

For best results in choosing a freshman class, take a high school transcript and stir in a measured dose of SAT or ACT scores, maybe both. Garnish with a couple of recommendation letters and serve. That's pretty much the recipe that comes out of the major testing companies and has been coming from them for generations. If high school grades are somewhat better predictors of first-year college grades than test scores, why not use them together and get the best of both worlds. (Bear in mind that the study we examined in the previous section dealt with graduate and professional schools.)

Sound sensible? We all want better decisions in college admissions. But how much better would they really be? A new study by Saul Geiser and Maria Santelices of the University of California tips the scale strongly in favor of high school GPA. Overall, their study arrived at three main conclusions: (1) high school grades are the *strongest* predictors of four-year college outcomes in all disciplines (the SAT II writing test was the next best); (2) high school grades perform better as predictors *after* the freshman year; and (3) relying on grades rather than test scores has *less adverse impact* on minority students.[14] But the researchers also looked at how much "value" the test scores might add to admissions decisions.

Geiser and Santelices had access to the four-year records of nearly 80,000 freshmen in the University of California system. This mother lode of data enabled them to examine outcomes other than first-year grades, which are chosen in part because they are easier to track. But we don't find the researchers' conclusions too surprising anyway. If test scores are good predictors of other test scores, and accomplishments are good predictors of later accomplishments, then why shouldn't grades be good predictors of subsequent grades? All of those "extraneous" things that grades take account of are clearly important for achievement in college, even if you can't easily test for them with paper and pencil. We mean things like performance in labs, writing papers (not in a single exam sitting), exploring topics in depth, participating in class, or performance on end-of-course tests.

Still, even when test scores, grades, parental education, family income, and the statewide rank of a student's high school are taken into account, just 27 percent of the variance in cumulative college grades can be predicted. That's making use of all the quantifiable data an admissions office would typically have. And 73 percent of the variance remains unexplained even then. Geiser and Santelices explain what this means in a way that's easier to get your mind around. If using *all the quantifiable predictor variables*, you project an individual applicant to have a cumulative GPA of 3.0 and you want to be 95 percent sure of that prediction, your possible error is quite large: ±0.79 grade points. That is, 95 percent of the time your applicant's cumulative college GPA will fall between 2.21 and 3.79: between C+ and A-. Not a very reassuring prediction for the admissions office to stake its freshmen class on, is it?

But how much of that meager prediction do the test scores (including both SAT I and SAT II) account for? Just 0.03 grade points. Removing the test scores from the equation expands the 95 percent confidence interval from ±0.79 to ±0.82! Still, some might argue that even so small an improvement is worth it. In a way, that's what the testing industry has been arguing for years. But you won't be surprised to learn that we don't quite see things that way. And we're not alone. More than eight hundred colleges have made the submission of college admission test scores optional, and that number continues to grow.[15] Is the cost in time, dollars, and energy really worth the minuscule increase in accuracy that is represented by 0.03 grade points?

FairTest's Schaeffer, whom we quoted above, frequently tells the following story. When speaking to gatherings of college admissions officers, he asks how many of their schools use (even if they don't require) SAT scores in making admissions decisions. (For more on colleges using but not requiring admissions test scores, see the sidebar "The Underside of Test Optional.") Nearly every hand in the room goes up in response. Then he asks the stunner, "How many would do so if the university had to pay the fees?" He's still waiting for the first hand to go up.[16]

To us that says a great deal. It says that, in the opinion of college admissions officers, the $45 charge for the basic SAT Reasoning Test isn't worth the minimal increase in the accuracy of predicting a student's success in college. Without SAT scores, colleges would have to make admission decisions based on grades, recommendations, and a more nuanced evaluation of a student's potential for success. That would mean placing more weight on those "nonacademic accomplishments" that Baird's study suggested were the best predictors of later accomplishment. And we believe that's likely to lead to decisions that are better in the long run at predicting career and life success, which should be our goals for all our children.

And in the final analysis, that's what Baird's study was trying to determine. He wanted to know what test scores, grades, and accomplishments can tell us about future success in a range of areas. But human lives are complex, and our forecasts about how they will turn out will be better if we are better at taking more of that complexity into account. Here's psychometrician and researcher Rebecca Zwick's take on the matter:

> A 1985 review of the literature on the prediction of career accomplishments [Baird's study] concluded that "across a rather large spectrum of the population, both test scores and grades tend to have modest predictive power for many kinds of 'later-life contributions.'" Based on information that has accumulated to date, this assessment seems a bit too rosy. For each study that shows a relationship, another does not. How well, then, do admissions test scores predict eventual career success? Overall, the answer appears to be, "not very well." An equally accurate answer might be "better than expected." After all, a test is just a small sample of a candidate's skills. It is extremely limited both in duration and in breadth—a point often emphasized by test critics. Career success, on the other hand, depends on many factors that are unrelated to competence, including health, family situation, and national economic conditions, not to mention luck.[17]

You can guess how it warmed our hearts to see that Zwick mentioned not just the sampling issue—both content and time—that has plagued standardized tests for a century, but also the matter of luck. As long as we're willing to accept a one-time sample of a student's performance as an indicator of how well that student will perform on any given day in a wide range of academic subjects and settings—to say nothing of performance in later life and career—luck will play a larger role in our decisions than most of us would be comfortable with.

How much of that 73 percent of the variance in cumulative college grades that *all predictor variables together* don't explain can be attributed to luck—good or bad—and how much can be explained by statistical anomalies, such as a restricted range of test takers? We can't say. Nor can anyone else, though researchers offer estimates, as Kuncel and Hezlett did. But whenever someone compares the test scores of different groups of students and infers what small differences have to say about the future performance of *individuals*, ask this: Where are those students' individual distributions of scores? Where are Rachel's one hundred SAT scores? And one thousand would be even better.

Of course, students don't have that many scores, but colleges are admitting real students, each of whom would produce a personal range of scores. And high schools are denying diplomas to individual students, not to group averages. As long as our tests are based on small samples of a broad domain and on similarly small samples of an individual's performance, having enough scores to create an individual distribution is the best—if highly impractical—way to minimize the role that plain old dumb luck plays in our educated guesses about future performance. It's also the reason every psychometrician and the major psychometric associations counsel against placing too much weight on an individual test score.[18] And it's the primary reason that absolute cut scores for important decisions are such a bad idea.

THE UNDERSIDE OF TEST OPTIONAL

Just because a college is "test optional" doesn't necessarily mean that it won't look at and use admissions test scores if students submit them. Note that Bob Schaeffer's story about who pays the bill for the tests acknowledges as much. But you would assume that the "use" he refers to has to do with selecting a freshman class. But there's more to it than that.

As we were researching this chapter, the *New York Times* ran a story examining the "marketing and competitive" purposes for which colleges use admissions test scores. It turns out that some "test optional" colleges require admissions test scores of those students who wish to be considered for merit-based scholarships. So they're saying to students: you don't have to submit your scores, unless you want a scholarship. The *Times* article says admissions directors at test-optional schools that don't engage in such practices are incredulous:

> "You can't say, 'Tests are not a good tool in the process,' and then say, 'If you don't submit you can't qualify for merit aid,'" says Debra Shaver, director of admission at Smith, which just admitted its first freshmen class under its test-optional program.*

The institutions that engage in this dubious use of the scores that they "don't require" partly justify their actions by saying they hope to attract larger numbers of high-scoring, high-achieving students. But the tests don't actually predict achievement in college very well, and the

---

* Lynne O'Shaughnessy, "The Other Side of 'Test Optional,'" *New York Times*, 20 July 2009.

colleges know that. That's why they dropped the requirement in the first place. What other purposes might be served?

How about trying to improve a school's position on those college ranking lists? Whenever a college goes test-optional, the number of applications it receives spikes for at least a few years, which means the school can be more selective and accept a smaller percentage of applicants—one of the criteria for moving up on the ranking lists. Moreover, at least some of the schools report to those who do the ranking the test scores they do receive, which tend to be higher both because they are voluntarily submitted and because those in competition for scholarships based on test scores will have higher-than-average scores as well. That's another criterion in the rankings.

It strains credulity to accept as innocent the actions of these colleges that are trying to have it both ways. These are not the poorly informed actions of middle-class parents from middle America. Those who run the admissions offices of our colleges and universities know full well what they are doing. Go test optional and increase minority applications, which should improve your minority enrollment—and move you up the rankings. But require tests for merit awards, thereby increasing the number of high-scorers who apply and submit their scores—and moving you up the rankings. Then publish the average test scores of students who submit test scores and are disproportionately not minority and disproportionately in contention for academic awards—which raises your average score and moves you up the list.

Smith College's admission director whom we quoted above continued, "I don't want to pass judgment on the institutions, but it doesn't make sense." Yes, it does, and go ahead and pass judgment. While the actions might seem self-contradictory, they make perfect sense. You just have to be more cynical in how you view some of the practices surrounding the "business" of college admissions.

—PLH and BMS

For all our efforts to make our predictions scientific—or at least to give that illusion through the use of a numerical scale—the complexity of the questions we wish to answer overwhelms both us and the testing technology we have relied on. We are not that far removed from the readers of tea leaves or crystal balls. And the question of what standardized tests predict—other than scores on other tests—must remain largely unanswered.

In our final two chapters, we move from the basic assumptions that underlie the tests themselves and the uses to which we put them. Instead, in chapter 10 we first look at two proposals for building an accountability system that lives up to its name, and in chapter 11 we examine the possibilities of a public school system that lives up to its history.

Ⓐ Ⓑ Ⓒ Ⓓ

A SMOKE SCREEN, LARRY BARBER

In the 1970s and 1980s, as a district-level administrator in charge of research, I worked with superintendents in one major city that was undergoing a difficult desegregation and in one smaller city that was not. We found test scores very useful.

As administrators, we served three main constituencies: elected officials (from the school board to the governor), the press (newspapers and TV), and the public (taxpayers, with and without kids in the schools). All three groups were clamoring for something simple and repeatable to use to judge how well their schools were doing. They believed that standardized test scores were that something. They thought the data could be sliced up in all sorts of ways to show how each school was doing and compare it to others in the district and to those in other cities and states. Some of the interest in test scores was about having bragging rights for their own schools or using the scores to justify kicking some butts.

More than once, I explained to the legislators and the news editors, as clearly and simply as I could, that standardized test scores were just too haphazard a measure to tell them whose school was better. What's more, if you didn't aggregate the scores, they were almost totally unreliable; if you did aggregate them, you washed out what little information they contained. In short, they were a waste of good money that could have been better spent on interesting and innovative efforts to improve instruction, which could then be evaluated in all sorts of ways that could help you decide what to do next. But no one wanted to hear that.

But the scores were very useful in enabling me to mislead the politicians, the press, and the public. I know that sounds awful, but I just gave them what they insisted on having. The benefit to me was that I could then pursue other kinds of research that actually made sense. The test scores were a *smoke screen* that gave the districts I worked for the cover they needed so they could go about the business of giving kids a better education.

Think of it as throwing a piece of steak to a watchdog so you can slip past him. The news media pounced on the data like hungry dogs, and the more we gave them, the hungrier they got. And while their attention was focused on the scores, we did our work, trying out new programs, evaluating them, and working to improve teaching and learning. All of this was made possible by the cover provided by the standardized test data.

So we used the scores to satisfy the people who wanted them and didn't know the difference between bad data and good data. But here's the important part: *they didn't want to know.* They resisted all explanations of why the tests were just the wrong way to go about evaluating the work of the schools.

But I can tell you this: *I never used the test data to make decisions about students.* Doing that would have been an exercise in stupidity that I couldn't bring myself to undertake. I don't know how I would deal with that problem if I were working in the schools today, but that's one reason that I'm not.

Larry Barber, former director of research for two urban school districts, was director of the Center for Evaluation, Development, and Research at Phi Delta Kappa International.

10

New Ideas for Genuine Accountability

Educators should be wary of allowing data or research to substitute for good judgment.

—Frederick Hess, 2009

It is surprising that so many education policy makers have been seduced into thinking that simple quantitative measures like test scores can be used to hold schools accountable for achieving complex educational outcomes.

—Richard Rothstein, Rebecca Jacobsen, and Tamara Wilder

Ask any elementary school teacher these days what comes to mind when she hears the word *accountability*, and we're betting that one of the first words you'll hear in reply is *testing*. The response is both understandable and unfortunate. It's understandable because, since No Child Left Behind became the law of the land in 2002, testing has come to dominate nearly every aspect of public schooling. (What's more, as we pointed out in chapter 1, the "blueprint" put forth by the Obama administration in March 2010 isn't likely to change this situation much.) And that teacher's response is unfortunate because true accountability means so much more.

There's an old story most readers will recognize from after-dinner speeches at clubs and community organizations. It's the one about the drunk staggering aimlessly in the circle of light surrounding a lamppost, scanning the same circle of pavement again and again.

"What are you doing?" a helpful passerby asks.
"Looking for my car keys," answers the drunk.

"Did you drop them somewhere around here?"

"I don't think so," replies the drunk.

"Then why look here?" the puzzled would-be helper wonders.

"It's the only place where there's any light."

We're surely not the first to employ this tale, not even the first to use it as a commentary on the shortsightedness of seeing standardized testing as a cure-all for the ills of education. But we think it carries even more significance when seen as a cautionary tale about our broader system of school account-ability. Could some of the most important things we want to know about our schools and the development of the young people in them lie outside that circle of light?

Asking that question brings us to the basic assumption about the use of standardized testing that we wish to examine in this chapter: *Standardized test scores tell citizens what they need to know about their schools.* As we argued in chapter 1, that's all school accountability really *ought* to mean: Citizens and their elected officials learn what they need to know about their schools.

In chapter 7 we considered the kind of narrowing of the curriculum that a strict regimen of high-stakes testing necessarily enforces. We said we didn't recall being invited to "the national discussion of the appropriate mix of sub-jects in our schools" because no such discussion ever took place.[1] This time, as we peer into the darkness outside that circle of light, our questions are broader and not so much technical as political and philosophical. And exam-ining them requires us to do some thinking about what we typically mean by accountability and what we might want that term to mean.

Like nearly everything about a complicated social organization such as our schools, accountability is multifaceted. But you wouldn't know that if all you did was read today's newspapers. Take our local paper as an example. Here's the headline of a recent release of scores on our state's accountability test, the ISTEP+: "MCCSC Fails Test for Second Year in a Row."[2] Well that settles it then. Our entire local school district just failed—and not for the first time. If that seems hard to explain in a university community located smack in the country's midsection that has always thought pretty well of its school system, it should. It doesn't actually make sense. But it does explain why the urge is so overwhelming to hold someone, somewhere responsible for such an outrageous evasion of duty—even if it is illusory.

What's going on? Partly, you have an artifact of a really Byzantine sys-tem of accountability that is focused almost exclusively on such quantitative outcomes as test scores, dropout rates, and attendance. At the same time, that system pays almost no attention to such processes as how students and teachers learn; how students learn about conflict resolution, cooperation, or collaboration; or how well the community engages with the school. Consider this. In 2006, when our local school system last made Adequate Yearly Progress (AYP), and in the following two years, when it "failed" to do so, the combined "report card" for the district shows that it met its numerical goals in a total of ninety-seven of ninety-nine areas in which data were collected. That doesn't seem a lot like "failure." The district missed AYP in 2007 *only* in "special education attendance at the high school level." In 2008, the district missed the goal *only* for the "free lunch English/language arts" subgroup.

Now, no one says that learning to use English well isn't important for low-income kids or that attendance isn't important for special education kids in high school. What's more, knowing where current trouble spots are located in the system can help us work to fix them. That's an appropriate role for an accountability system. But allowing a "failure" in these two data cells to label our school district a "failure" is a prime example of what Rick Hess of the American Enterprise Institute, an outfit not known for being softheaded or given to bleeding-heart liberalism, has called "the new stupid." Here's Hess:

> Today's enthusiastic embrace of data has waltzed us directly from a petulant resistance to performance measures to a reflexive and unsophisticated reliance on a few simple metrics—namely, graduation rates, expenditures, and the reading and math test scores of students in grades three through eight. The result has been a pirouette from one troubling mind-set to another; we have quickly pivoted from the "old stupid" to the "new stupid."[3]

Hess sees the characteristics of this "new stupid" playing out in the use of data in half-baked ways, translating research simplistically, and not paying enough attention to "management" data (the kind of information that has to do with operations, hiring, and finances of running a school system). His number-one suggestion for avoiding the "new stupid" is that "educators should be wary of allowing data or research to substitute for good judgment."

In the local example we've cited, we can certainly see a half-baked understanding of the test data that has been allowed to override common sense and has led to a declaration of failure for our schools. What's more, the "standards" that many schools and districts failed to meet in 2008 are set to be ratcheted up by fixed percentages each year until 2014.

Of course, now we have a new federal administration, and it has proposed doing away with the 2014 deadline for proficiency. Surely, that's a good thing, no? To which we reply, "Yes, but. . . ." The big "but" is that the "blueprint" set out by President Obama and Secretary Duncan adopts the same approach to accountability as its predecessors did. The 2014 deadline has been replaced with a "target" (they say it's not an absolute deadline) that by 2020 all students (here we go again with "all students") will be "college and career ready." But the same misunderstanding of accountability plagues the new proposal. That is, "college and career ready" still relies on annual testing in grades three through eight and once during high school; still relies on rewards for success (i.e., high test scores) and "interventions" for persistent failure (i.e., low test scores); and still fails to address the fundamental social, cultural, and familial issues that strongly influence students' performance. But "interventions" are so much nicer than "sanctions," don't you think?

But let us return to NCLB, which remains the law of the land as we write. You may feel free to substitute 2020 for 2014 in the paragraphs that follow. Very little else seems likely to change.

In the magical year of 2014, the federal government has declared that all children in all subgroups will be "proficient" in reading, math, and science; will show up every day for school (at least 95 percent attendance); and will overcome all those troublesome learning difficulties that educators allegedly keep trotting out to excuse their own poor performance. Of course, it goes without saying that such exemplary children will also be "college and career ready."

The absurdity of requiring 100 percent proficiency (taken to mean the equivalent of all students meeting the very high NAEP proficiency levels) should have been patently obvious to those who gave us NCLB. But our policy makers generally overlook such obvious impediments, and they compound the absurdity when they pretend that they can magically legislate away the impact of poverty on children and their learning or when they act as if the "special" part of special education is nothing more than a distinction without a difference.

Here's an addendum we'd like to propose. Also in 2014 or 2020, let's change the road signs at the entrance to every town in the country to read "Entering Lake Wobegon." Our fixation with a single kind of accountability has reached such a level of silliness that proposing 100 percent proficiency barely seems far-fetched. At times like these, we're driven to consult the great sages, and occupying a place of honor among that tribe is Pete Hogwallop of the Coen brothers' film *O Brother, Where Art Thou?* When he finds himself purposely confused by his fast-talking partner Everett, Pete sums up the sensible person's response to confronting such utter lunacy: "That don't make *no* sense!" he wails. And 100 percent proficiency for everyone on every scale don't make no sense to us, neither! What are we to make of such silliness? We say make fun of it! It is, as Hess terms it, a completely "half-baked use of data." And in such cases, it is absolutely okay to point and stare at the emperor's nakedness.

But the future of our young people and our nation is at stake, so once we've had a little levity at the expense of some sober-faced if feather-brained policy makers, we need to get serious about this accountability thing. We need to initiate that national discussion that we so badly need to have.

VOICES CRYING IN THE WILDERNESS

It's not like some educators and policy analysts haven't been trying to initiate a national conversation on school accountability that examines our current system and seeks better alternatives. We'd like to share brief synopses of two proposals we've noted in the past few years.

A few years back, Ken Jones of the University of Southern Maine borrowed some thinking about accountability from the business world and adapted it to education.[4] He posed three basic questions: For *what* should schools be held accountable? To *whom* should they render account? and *How* should they do so? In answer to the first question Jones lists five areas for which schools should expect to be held accountable at the very least. We repeat them with our brief comments:

- *The physical and emotional well-being of students.* Because schools do care for our youngsters for nearly half their waking hours, this one seems like a no-brainer. If you're not physically healthy or if you're troubled emotionally, you won't be in any condition to learn much. This in no way implies that teachers are in a position to fix all of children's physical or emotional problems, but schools can certainly follow the physician's oath of "first, do no harm" and at the same time seek to provide all the support in this area that they can.
- *Student learning.* Jones construes learning broadly, so that it includes knowledge of subject matter, but also "skills and dispositions needed in a modern democratic society." Schools on their own can't guarantee specific outcomes in this area, but working with parents, students, and other community members, they can see that the broad educational needs of the community are taken into account.
- *Teacher learning.* We've all heard lately that teachers are crucial to student learning, so it makes sense to make self-improvement for staff members something schools should focus on. Mostly, this involves providing time, which translates into money, of course, if only because more teachers will need to be hired so that teachers can work together and visit one another's classes in order to learn with their colleagues.

- *Equity and access*. No, schools shouldn't be expected to solve all the social problems of the entire society. But that doesn't mean they shouldn't try. Jones puts it this way: "Our press for excellence must include a press for fairness." We try to teach fairness to our kindergartners. Maybe it's time we listened to what we are saying.
- *Improvement*. Because schools need to be learning organizations for both students and staff, it's important that their efforts at self-assessment and improvement be nurtured. Complex human organizations will improve only when the people directly involved work together to pursue common goals and make changes happen. Policy makers can't legislate that kind of mind-set; at best, they can help create the conditions that make it possible.

In our current accountability schemes, the only one of these five areas that gets much purchase is student learning. Though some rumblings about "improvement" and "growth models" have been heard of late, they're largely unformed and still saddled with all the limitations that plague all test-score-driven plans that focus primarily on outcomes. Indeed, the new "blueprint" requires teachers to be judged, at least in part, by their students' "growth."[5] Anyone willing to bet that student growth under Obama's plan will be measured by anything other than the same broken tool of test scores? You won't get good odds betting against that one.

But teacher learning? We have universities for that; schools aren't responsible. Emotional and physical well-being of students? That's the job of families and religious institutions; it's not how we're going to judge schools. Access and equity? State and federal laws cover those.

To whom should schools be accountable? To their primary clients, which are *decidedly not* the federal or state governments. By Jones's reasoning, with which we concur, the primary clients of schools are students, parents, and the local community, and it is these groups that should be empowered to make decisions about both the means and the ends of education, with perhaps a few checks from higher levels of government to ensure equity and adherence to professional standards.

How to hold schools accountable? This one will be much more complicated in Jones's system than our current practice of just pouring truckloads of test scores into a series of spreadsheets to see if a school or district fails to reach an arbitrary numerical target. And to judge by our local experience, ninety-seven bull's-eyes hit out of ninety-nine aimed for just turns out not to be good enough for Adequate Yearly Progress. In the "balanced model" of accountability that Jones argues for, we see that "states and districts are jointly responsible with schools and communities for student learning.

Reciprocal accountability is needed: One level of the system is responsible to the others, and all are responsible to the public."[6] And all of that communication involves multiple measures that take account of both local contexts and professional standards. Jones is adamant—and we surely agree—that "a standardized approach toward school accountability cannot work in a nation as diverse as the U.S."[7] At least, it can't work without creating a great deal of "collateral damage," much of which has been our subject matter in the previous chapters.

The overall purpose of such an accountability system is not to punish or reward schools or to declare them successes or failures (this isn't a sports league) but to improve the learning of students and teachers and to provide information and guidance for local decision making. Along the way, we have a chance to put the principles of our democratic system of government to work as we balance the responsibility and power appropriately among the levels of government.

An even more comprehensive proposal for an improved accountability system was put forth in a 2008 book-length presentation by economist Richard Rothstein of the Economic Policy Institute and his coauthors, Rebecca Jacobsen of Michigan State University and Tamara Wilder of the University of Michigan.[8] It's even more difficult for us to give a thumbnail sketch of their plan than it was for Jones's proposal, but there are important points of similarity worth emphasizing, not least of which is the focus on what schools should be accountable for.

Rothstein and his colleagues begin with an analysis of the goals of schooling as Americans have expressed them throughout history. They arrive at eight broad goals, which we present below in skeletal format. The authors also commissioned a survey that asked the general public, local school board members, and state legislators to assign a relative importance to each of the eight goals, with the total adding to 100 percent. (The figures in parentheses are the authors' combined weighting of the rankings of these three groups, and the groups were remarkably similar in their overall rankings to begin with.) Our brief comments follow each goal:

 Basic academic knowledge and skills (21 percent). This one really is a no-brainer. Even if they had the time, many parents don't feel comfortable teaching their children the full range of academic knowledge and skills, so helping kids acquire academic knowledge and skills must be a school responsibility. What we find striking is how *low* this percentage is. Given our national intoxication with test scores in math and reading, we would have thought somewhere around 50 percent might have been more likely. Then again, maybe this just shows something we have long suspected: People in general are smarter than their leaders give them credit for.

- *Critical thinking and problem solving* (16 percent). Even competent adults who routinely solve complex problems in their work and lives don't always feel confident about teaching their children how to do so. But they do recognize that this goal is important, and it reaches second place.
- *Social skills and work ethic* (13 percent). These include such things as communication skills, a sense of personal responsibility, and the ability to get along with others from different backgrounds. Curiously, every time employers are asked what's missing from the high school graduates—and, yes, even college graduates—that they hire each year, they point to these kinds of skills. Most such skills have only a slim academic component, but then most of our daily lives, even at work, have only a slim academic component.
- *Citizenship and community responsibility* (13 percent). This set of outcomes encompasses such things as public ethics, knowledge of how government works, and participation in community life through voting, volunteering, and so on. If we go back to the Founders of the republic—in particular, Jefferson and Franklin—we find that these outcomes are among the primary reasons that we have a school system today. And Horace Mann, regarded as the founder of the system of public schools that we know, concurred, though he did extend the purposes of schooling to encompass more of the eight goals Rothstein and his coauthors identify.
- *The appreciation of arts and literature* (10 percent). The hope is that children who learn to appreciate the great works of human culture will carry that appreciation into adulthood and will come to better understand the human condition by doing so. This doesn't mean that everyone must love *Silas Marner*. (How many fourteen-year-olds are swept up by a nineteenth-century novel that treats the moral redemption of a hardhearted old man?) Rather, all children *deserve* to be exposed early and often to the range of ways people express themselves. Then they will be able to find and develop the ones that best speak to them individually. Note the emphasis on "deserve" in the preceding sentence; it's important to understand that learning more than the basic skills encompassed by the current barren notion of AYP is every child's *right*, not something for the privileged few. The new "blueprint" does feature some competitive grants for innovations in the arts, history, drama, and other subject areas where tests are not required. But by virtue of being a competitive program, all schools won't be encouraged to devote significant time and

energy to these nontested areas. And because what's tested tends to be what's taught, not much is likely to change as a result.

- *Preparation for skilled work* (10 percent). This one includes all the skills that are directly transferable to life in the workplace. It would encompass everything from such general learning as how to search databases and how to use Excel or PowerPoint to the actual qualification and certification for jobs for those who don't attend college. And yes, there still are vocational programs that qualify students who choose them to enter a given trade.
- *Physical health* (9 percent). Children should learn about their health and nutrition and be encouraged to develop good habits in these areas. Learning to operate the equipment you come into the world with just seems to be a sensible goal for all our children. When more Americans than ever are obese and the costs of health care are skyrocketing, cutting back on health and physical education in favor of preparing for standardized tests of reading and math "don't make *no* sense."
- *Emotional health* (8 percent). This outcome includes developing self-confidence, respect for others, and the ability to resist pressure to engage in irresponsible behavior. It is closely related to the pursuit of physical health and just as important to overall well-being. The need to pursue this goal should be obvious to anyone who has ever watched the parade of stressed-out Americans who populate any weekday afternoon's talk shows.

Rothstein and his colleagues have also placed on the table for discussion a schematic for an accountability system that would enable schools to monitor and improve their performance on each of these goals. Briefly, their plan builds on the original design of the National Assessment of Educational Progress, which has never been implemented on its originally planned schedule or in all the nonacademic areas once envisioned. While some paper-and-pencil testing would certainly be appropriate in judging performance in each of the goal areas, other kinds of assessment would clearly be necessary. Standardized testing in the eight goal areas would be part of this more complex picture, but that testing would not need to examine every student, every year, on every item. It would sample populations, as NAEP has always done, and would be augmented by a system of regular and formal school inspections, similar to the systems used in many other nations and involving some extended observations and interviews of students and teachers in schools and classrooms.

The system Rothstein and his colleagues have outlined would not produce neat numbers that we could pin to every child's shirt so we could arrange them all in order or rank their teachers according to "effectiveness." But it would reflect the considered judgment of a trained corps of educators. Isn't that subjective, you ask? To a degree, yes, just as the choice of test content and format and proficiency levels is subjective. But what such observations offer that the tests don't is some opportunity to take account of a wider range of experiences and behaviors on the part of students and staff members and to do so in a range of settings over a longer period of time.

Unfortunately, for all its talk about getting rid of the bad parts of NCLB, the "blueprint" put out by the Obama Department of Education is thoroughly infatuated with the notion of "effectiveness." By our hand count, the words *effective, effectiveness*, and *effectively* appear eighty-three times in a document that is just thirty-nine pages of heavily illustrated text with wide margins. And all of these effective schools and effective teachers who are to be singled out for rewards are to be selected, at least in part, by students' test scores. We believe the "part" that test scores play in these selections will be the leading role.

As always, the devil is in the details of any accountability plan for a public institution as complex as public education. And we certainly don't mean to imply that the proposal by Rothstein and his coauthors should be adopted as is. Nor do they. For instance, we are less hopeful than they are about how well our system of school accreditation will morph into the kind of inspectorate they hope for. But we do commend them for doing just what needs to be done in a democracy: putting an idea forward for public comment, revision, and improvement. Ultimately, doing so will let everyone have a say and will help our schools be accountable to us for all the outcomes and processes we all care about. We should then be in a better position to make reasoned decisions about our schools than we are today, when everything about a school's "performance" is bundled into a single number that masks as much information as it reveals.

All good parents work to help their own children achieve in every one of the eight outcome areas Rothstein and his colleagues focus on. From the historical information they muster, as well as from their survey data, most people—including our school boards and political leaders—would like to support these goals for everyone's children. Why then do we find it so easy to let some of them go unmonitored and so unnoticed? How can we allow test scores in just a couple of areas to dominate our thinking and skew our judgment as to whether or not a school is doing good work? To a large extent, the reason is a failure of trust coupled with an unquestioned faith in the infallibility of numbers (see chapter 4) and an unwillingness to put our resources where our survey responses are.

TRUST BUT VERIFY

Back in the days of the Cold War, one of the things Ronald Reagan was famous for was the line "trust but verify." He was referring to the former Soviet Union and the problem of satisfying ourselves that its promises to reduce nuclear weapons were being kept. It was natural that our view of a nation whose leaders had promised just two decades earlier to "bury" us would be less than trusting. But in spelling out the dilemma of arms reduction, President Reagan also inadvertently put his finger on the two main desires that motivate school accountability. While we may trust that what happens in our schools is what we want to happen, we want to *know* that it is so. We need to verify. Considered in this light, today's school accountability efforts are badly out of balance. They have swung sharply toward the "verify" side, and we need to restore the balance.

How do we do that? The first thing we need to accept is that we must extend a measure of trust to those who provide public services. There is actually no choice about this. The only question is how to determine that our trust is well placed without getting in the way of those very service providers. We can't all ride along on every run of the local fire truck, or the whole town will soon be in cinders.

But trust is more central to the connection between the public and its schools than is true of many other public services. Complex services whose outcomes can be determined only years later *always* depend on higher levels of trust.[9] Therefore, it makes sense—and goes a long way toward giving all of us some peace of mind—if our accountability system for such complex, long-term services is a multifaceted one. That accountability system needs to take into account as many sources of information of as many kinds as possible. Some sources will be simple scorecard material, such as attendance figures, number of field trips, or the disposition of the district's capital budget. Others will be more subjective, but often richer and more detailed, such as your impression of the dedication of student service club members when they show up to help clean up after a storm.

Compare your local water company to your local schools. Certainly, clean water is important and so is appropriate waste disposal, but the accountability issue for the water company is in many ways a simpler one. When you see the coliform bacteria count, you don't have to wait thirty years to find out whether it was accurate and the water is safe. Just open the tap, fill a glass, drink, and wait. You'll have feedback shortly.

When the schools publish average standardized test scores in math and reading and claim that their students are learning what they need to know to be successful in the twenty-first century, you're going to need to know considerably more before you accept that conclusion. You and your children don't have thirty years to stand around waiting to see how good those predictions turn out to be. You'll want to know what the teacher thinks are your child's strengths and weaknesses as a learner—in all subjects, not just reading and math; you'll want to know how well the high school musical came off this past spring; you'll want to know how the school is meeting the needs of the kids from immigrant communities; and the list could be extended indefinitely.

And that's exactly the point. In standardized testing for accountability, we have come to accept a snapshot of our schools when a full-featured boxed DVD set wouldn't even give us a complete picture. We quoted Ken Jones above: "A standardized approach toward school accountability cannot work in a nation as diverse as the U.S." Even people from the same ethnic backgrounds and social classes are simply too variable and too individual in their desires and goals to give a fair accounting of themselves on a single measure. When we mix in a medley of races and cultures, matters only become more complicated. Following a similar line of thought, Rothstein and his colleagues hark back to economics Nobelist Herbert Simon's early days as a junior researcher when he was examining the full range of municipal services. Both they and Simon conclude that complex "public services have goals that can't be easily defined in simple numerical terms."[10] They put their frustration (and ours) this way:

> It is surprising that so many education policy makers have been seduced into thinking that simple quantitative measures like test scores can be used to hold schools accountable for achieving complex educational outcomes. After all, similar accountability systems have been attempted, and have been found lacking, in other sectors, both private and public, many times before.[11]

The accountability system we need for our schools must be complex, nuanced, and flexible. We are accountable for what we are responsible for, and there's plenty of responsibility to go around. Among the happiest phrases we've encountered in researching this chapter is Jones's term "reciprocal accountability." We'd like to expand it beyond his use to describe the relations between schools and communities and districts and states.

We think there are many roles for everyone where accountability is concerned, beginning with students. Here's just a thumbnail view of how deeply into our society real accountability for learning extends.

Students are responsible for doing their best. It's that simple—and that hard. Every single one of us slacks off on occasion, but that doesn't make it right—for parents, teachers, or students. But in order for students to do their best and show what they can do, they need help. It is a *reciprocal* accountability system, after all.

Parents must be accountable for providing—as their circumstances allow—good nutrition, a focus on learning, a place to study, and sometimes a sympathetic ear. Parents are also their children's first teachers, and that responsibility doesn't end when kindergarten begins. Parents are also responsible for keeping in touch with teachers and schools. Any health problems children have should be communicated to the school nurse and teacher, and emotional traumas (e.g., the family dog died this weekend) and triumphs (e.g., Bobby is no longer a Tenderfoot in the Boy Scouts) should be passed along as well.

Teachers must work to keep students learning. Sounds simple, but it's far from it. It can involve helping to find the books that will excite students' interest or helping to find someone in the community to help students answer their pressing questions. Say a kindergartner asks, "What happens to my 'business' when I flush?" That's probably not in this week's lesson plan, but we can practically guarantee that seeking an answer will yield at least a week's worth of valuable "exploration" that cuts across science, language arts, social studies, and math. No predetermined syllabus can match the serendipity of student-driven interest, and no commercially prepared curriculum can anticipate where that interest will emerge. Teachers must be alert to these opportunities and flexible enough to take advantage of them when they arise. Neither of these essential characteristics of good teachers—or, as the "blueprint" would have it, "effective" teachers—can be captured by standardized tests given to students or, for that matter, even by tests given to teachers themselves.

School administrators at the building level are responsible for keeping the campus safe and secure and for fostering a sense that the whole school is a community in its own right. That can mean organizing and boosting volunteer and service efforts or making time to celebrate successes and mourn losses. But administrators are also responsible for supporting teachers' efforts to help students learn. This can involve everything from tinkering with schedules to issuing passes on short notice to making good use of "teacher training days" to turning up funds for a special class set of supplemental novels because one junior English class has "discovered" Virginia Woolf. It can also mean, as one of our former colleagues was prone to put it, absorbing as much b.s. from the central office as possible, though if everyone plays the appropriate part in a real accountability system, there won't be nearly as much of that b.s. landing on a principal's desk.

Education officials at the district, state, and even federal levels are responsible for helping those who come to school every day—both staff and students—to do their jobs well. That could mean working to equalize funding or finding help for English language learners, and it includes gathering data of all sorts, including test data when it's appropriate. But officials up and down the bureaucracy of education should be circumspect in drawing sensible inferences from the data they collect. While it won't be possible for their interpretations to always be correct, it's important that they understand that the aim of collecting data and drawing conclusions is to enable those in schools and communities to do their jobs better.

We could expand any one of these paragraphs on the groups that are accountable for education, or we could extend the list through political leaders, spiritual leaders, business leaders, and so on. But the point is that, if it "takes a village" to rear a child, that village is larger and more interconnected today than ever before. That means that watching over its efforts—a more nurturing way of saying keeping it accountable—is a more complex task than ever before.

It seems we've always known intuitively that the goals of our education system were multifaceted. Certainly, the historical analysis that Rothstein and his coauthors present, as well as the results of the survey they commissioned, support that notion. Our current test-dominated accountability system is anything but multifaceted, and in the next, and final, chapter we look in detail at how our narrow focus on test scores has caused us to forget the primary reasons we have a public school system in the first place. We as a nation seem destined to keep forgetting. We're here to remind you.

Ⓐ Ⓑ Ⓒ Ⓓ
THE GAME OF SCHOOL, KEN JONES

Even though I was good at taking them, I have never had much use for standardized tests—not as a student, or a teacher, or a teacher educator. I think that they serve primarily to identify the winners and losers in the game of school, that they are inherently rigged to favor the mainstream middle- and upper-class white culture, and that they are biased with respect to learning styles and intelligences. My suspicion is that whether you think standardized tests can be useful depends on whether you're a hammer or a nail in our society. Do you do the pounding or do you get pounded?

Do these tests tell the truth? If not, how useful can they be? In the way they are now used for high-stakes decisions about students and teachers, they have been corrupted, probably irretrievably. The pressure to get good scores promotes gamesmanship and drilling more than learning.

Do the tests have any potential for helping teaching and learning? Maybe, if you believe that knowing how one child compares to others on a flawed measuring device can help a teacher know what to do with all the different children in her room. Maybe, if you think that the kind of knowledge and thinking they test for is crucial in the real world. Maybe, if you think children should be sorted, teachers should be compliant, and policy makers need numbers to justify how to spend money on schools.

Might they be useful for the sake of evaluating a curriculum? Possibly trend lines and disaggregated data could help identify strengths and weaknesses. Maybe they could work the way the National Assessment of Educational Progress used to operate: no arbitrary cut scores to identify "proficiency" and results not used as political weapons. But I still question how such information helps an individual teacher with her instruction. For me, that is what matters most.

Let's reframe the question. Don't ask if the tests can be useful, but rather how useful they can be for improving teaching and learning, especially as compared to other things we could do with the megabucks that go toward testing. At the top of my list is investing in teacher understanding and skills in conducting valid classroom assessments and setting up systems of peer review to monitor and improve such professional practices. Invest in people and trust in people, not in corporate technological solutions.

My comments, like the standardized tests themselves, might not be very useful. But they are certainly more honest.

Ken Jones is an associate professor of teacher education at the University of Southern Maine, Portland.

11

What's It All About?

From the standpoint of society, education is a preparation of children for
adult life as adults in their society conceive it.

—Herb Childress, 2006, quoting John Ogbu

Tax-supported public schools in the United States were not established
150 years ago to ensure jobs for graduates. . . .

—Larry Cuban, 2009

Everyone has heard the old saying, "If it ain't broke, don't fix it." But surely
somewhere there's a corollary—unspoken because folk wisdom deems some
things too obvious for words—that would go like this: "If it is broke, stop
using it." We think the system of testing and accountability in the United
States is clearly "broke." The unintended consequences of our overuse and
misuse of standardized tests have overwhelmed any potential benefit. Yet we
watch in stunned disbelief as, rather than putting down this broken tool, our
politicians and policy makers continue to flail away with it. In doing so, they
simply make a bad situation that much worse.

In this book we've examined the tool of standardized testing as we now use it
to judge our students, our teachers, our schools, and our school systems. We've
structured the chapters around examining some of the basic assumptions that
underlie the tests themselves and the ways we use them. And in the previous
chapter, we looked at two new proposals for building a system of accountability
that is better than the one we currently have or the minimally revised version
being touted by the Obama administration. It was necessary to do this, to go
through this process, so that you would understand that many of the messages

you have been getting about the performance of students and schools—even when they come from well-intentioned people and are backed by pages of numbers—are distorted, overly narrow, and generally incomplete.

We've not explicitly examined the job the schools are trying to do in the first place, but in the end, the evaluation of our schools must be done in the context of the purpose they are intended to achieve. This was the point we made way back in chapter 1: Accountability tells you what's going on; evaluation follows and depends entirely on a judgment of purpose. What exactly do we want our schools to do? What is the primary purpose of the public schools, and how can we best help them meet that purpose? To answer this question, we'll need to ask why Americans have seen education as so important for so long, even before the founding of the nation. That will mean consulting both historical and contemporary figures—from Jefferson and Franklin to John Dewey and from John Goodlad and Deborah Meier to Steven Wolk.

A topic like the purpose of public education is big and squishy. Everything we read that's related to education seems to have something to say about its purpose, but true to our modus operandi throughout, we're going to pare down our list of secondary commentators to just a few, the ones we believe get closest to the essential truth about what public schools are for. But before we hear from the Founders or any contemporary education pundits, we thought we would start by asking people more like the rest of us: public school parents.

When we began this project, we asked a friendly neighborhood teacher to poll the parents of her third-graders and ask them about how they hoped their children would turn out a decade in the future, when they would have completed their years of compulsory schooling. She explicitly didn't ask *what* the parents wanted their kids to be, and in any case at age eighteen most kids won't have finished preparing for the adult role they will one day play in society. Instead, she asked parents *how* they wanted their children to turn out. It's an important distinction.

Think for a moment about what you might say in these parents' places. Suppose your child was a shiny new third-grader, just beginning the school year. How would you want that child to turn out in ten years? The number one attribute that these parents wanted their kids to exhibit when they were eighteen was some form of "confidence." They said they wanted confident, self-confident, and self-assured young people to emerge from their years of schooling.

Perhaps this has something to do with the age of the children, who hadn't been in school all that long and might still have been showing some leftover uneasiness about being there. But we don't think so. We think these parents know that people have got to believe in their own capacity if they're going to succeed, and they hope that the experiences the schools and the rest of society will provide their children throughout their formative years will develop this inner sense of efficacy.

But another desire was nearly as prevalent as the desire for confident children: Parents wanted their children to be kind. The words they used ranged from kind to generous to amiable to compassionate to empathetic. Like the desire for confident children, this goal was clearly social, not academic.

Academic goals weren't completely absent, of course, for we are talking about school. But explicitly academic goals—such as "successful in school" and "good reader/writer"—were mentioned by only a minority of parents, about the same number as mentioned some version of "happy" as a description of how they wanted their children to turn out.

Now we don't for a moment claim that this is a "scientific" poll. It's the ultimate sample of convenience, and we cite it only to jump-start our thinking—and yours. The parents of these kids read about the achievement of local schools in the newspaper, they compare the average test scores of the local elementary schools, they hear reports on outcomes of state testing programs, and they kvetch about how their kids are being prepared for the twenty-first century. Yet their hopes and expectations for the kind of people their children will be as young adults are weighted heavily toward social and personal goals, not academic or career goals.

So are their hopes and expectations in line with what has traditionally been expected of our public schools? Or is this just an aberration? Is it merely a reflection of a generation of parents who were reared during the late twentieth century, the alleged heyday of the "self-esteem movement"? Many swords were crossed at the close of the last century over just how real this "movement" was or how much of it was the result of a media-fanned frenzy. But we believe these parents are not mouthing empty platitudes so much as they genuinely recognize that a well-rounded education includes more than just academic skills, however important they may be.

Moreover, the views of these parents of twenty-first-century schoolchildren are in a direct line of descent from those of many who worked diligently to found the education system we have today. And they are also in step with some of the more progressive contemporary thinkers on the topic.

SCHOOLING FOR RULING

Every educator and many laypeople have heard the term *education for democracy*. Perhaps you are among them. If so, what the heck do you think it means? We're going to try to say, so bear with us for we're about to enter a thicket of abstractions, which we hope to be able to give some substance to.

We owe the delightfully rhyming title of this section to Deborah Meier, who refers to schooling for ruling as "the singular responsibility" of the public schools. But the thought behind schooling for ruling extends back to the ancient Greeks and Romans and took on its explicitly American cast during the Colonial Era. However, even after the Revolution, Meier notes that only a small elite typically received anything remotely resembling what we would recognize today as "an education." "Only the leisured," she explains, "had time for the tough intellectual work—and networking—that democracy rests on."[1] It's comforting to know that not all "networking" is about career success![2]

But "education for democracy" looms large in the nation's educational history and provides the central impetus for the founding of our public school system. Yet the idea is still not any easier to talk about today than it was hundreds of years ago.

Let's look back about as far as we can. Since the midseventeenth century, communities in many colonies, particularly in New England, had publicly funded schools. These schools weren't what we would consider public schools today. Their primary aim was religious instruction, with less emphasis on being able to understand the laws of the colony. Of course, acquiring literacy was always a central occupation for students and was necessary for serious Bible study. As early as 1647, in the quaintly named Olde Deluder Satan Act, Massachusetts required towns with more than fifty households to fund a school and pay a teacher, either through public or private funding. If the town had at least one hundred households, it was also required to have a secondary school that taught Greek and Latin. And it's well to recall that in the mid-seventeenth century, Massachusetts was for Europeans very much the frontier.

But by the eighteenth century, a broader, less sectarian set of goals had begun to emerge. Ben Franklin, in *Proposals Relating to the Education of Youth in Pensilvania* (Philadelphia, 1749), proposed a school with an inclusive curriculum. Not surprisingly, Franklin's proposed course of study had a practical slant, including handwriting, arithmetic/geometry, English grammar, a great deal of history (as much for its moral lessons as anything else), public speaking, astronomy, and geography.[3] The noted historian of education Lawrence Cremin summed up eighteenth-century American views, at least after the founding of the nation, as supporting the need for education that was appropriate to a republic. Whereas monarchies could educate for a class-bound society, "republics needed an education that would motivate all men to choose public over private interest."[4]

When we think of figures from American history who have been influential with regard to education, the first name that generally comes to mind is Thomas Jefferson, without a doubt the nation's first education president, even though that term didn't become popular until the 1980s. The importance of spurring citizens to play a role in public life was clearly on Jefferson's mind whenever the notion of "general education" was broached. Educational historian Jennings Wagoner sums up Jefferson's general view of education: "To Jefferson, education should equip *all* citizens of the new nation with the skills and sensibilities that would enable each to become self-sufficient, able to pursue happiness, and capable of maintaining a republican society."[5]

Though our third president is justly famous for founding the University of Virginia, he always had an ambitious vision for an entire system of education. And though his plans for a lower school system didn't bear fruit in his lifetime, in the Rockfish Gap Report he was able to spell out a set of objectives for a basic education, which included:

- To give every citizen the information he needs for the transaction of his own business;
- To enable him to calculate for himself, and to express and preserve his ideas, his contracts and accounts, in writing;
- To improve, by reading, his morals and faculties;
- To understand his duties to his neighbors and country, and to discharge with competence the functions confided to him by either;
- To know his rights; to exercise with order and justice those he retains; and to choose with discretion the fiduciary of those he delegates; and to notice their conduct with diligence, with candor, and judgment;
- And, in general, to observe with intelligence and faithfulness all the social relations under which he shall be placed.[6]

Note that both Jefferson and Franklin kept a clear eye on the public purpose for a public education system. While that purpose has endured over the centuries, its stock has fluctuated considerably, and, though it has not disappeared, most of us now take it for granted. It generates no test scores and no headlines.

Recently, Larry Cuban, an education historian, Stanford University professor, and former school superintendent, addressed this issue and the big questions that dangle tantalizingly from it in an article in *The American Prospect*. Cuban challenges the futile search for a one-size-fits-all kind of schooling that seems to drive our reform efforts. He writes:

Tax-supported public schools in the United States were not established 150 years ago to ensure jobs for graduates or to replace the family or church. They were established to make sure that children would grow into literate adults who respected authority and could make reasoned judgments, accept differences of opinions, and fulfill their civic duty to participate in the political and social life of their communities.[7]

More specifically, Cuban enumerates some of "desirable social attitudes, values, and behaviors" that many of us count on schools to help pass down to each successive generation. What attributes do citizens need to have if our democracy is to work? Cuban lists some:

- Open-mindedness to different opinions and a willingness to consider various points of view;
- Respect for values that differ from one's own;
- Treating individuals decently and fairly, regardless of background; and
- A commitment to "talk through" problems and openly discuss, reason, deliberate, and struggle toward compromise when disputes arise.

The job of citizen is a demanding one, and these civic goals of schooling, which are rarely addressed explicitly, are not easy to meet. They represent attitudes that young people need to observe and practice frequently if they are to become "proficient" in them. Nor are these attitudes any easier for us to maintain once we have moved into the adult world. Respect for the points of view of others? Open-mindedness? President Obama addressed this very matter directly in his 2009 commencement address at the University of Notre Dame. While the opposing camps on the abortion issue may in some sense be "irreconcilable," as the president said, he advised strongly against "reducing those with differing views to caricature."

Doesn't caricature aptly describe a lot of the policy-related debates surrounding schooling? or levels of taxation? or health care for all Americans? We have to say that all too often, it does. We hope that in the preceding chapters we've avoided caricaturing those who support standardized testing for accountability. Certainly, we've tried to give them their due—especially with regard to intentions. For we do believe that those of both political parties who wrote, voted for, and endorsed the No Child Left Behind Act are not demons. We certainly believe in the sincere good intentions of those now working on President Obama's "blueprint" for overhauling NCLB, though we are far from satisfied that the new plan is all that new or adequately addresses the flaws of its predecessor. We believe the aim of these policy makers, today and a decade ago, is to help America's children. What we have questioned are the means they've chosen, in particular the lever of high-stakes standardized testing.

BUT THAT'S NOT ALL

So if "schooling for ruling" in this republic of ours is the historical reason that the public schools exist, why not just refocus our efforts on civics and community service and be done with it? No more debates about testing for different purposes or the relative value of the arts and computer science. Let all children study the lives of the secular saints (the Founders, Lincoln, the Roosevelts, and others). Then we'll tell them, "Go thou and do likewise." Case closed.

Like everything else involving humans and their incredible brains, it's not so simple. "Education" is much broader than schooling, and even schooling has multiple aims. We have so far focused on "schooling for democratic citizenship" because of its historical prominence and because it is so frequently overlooked and taken for granted. Given the obsessive focus in recent years on academic test scores—almost exclusively in math and reading—this important aim of the schools is being seriously eroded. But the schools have other legitimate aims, as well.

We like the breakdown of goals for schooling that John Goodlad provided way back in 1979. Goodlad devoted a short monograph to exploring the purposes of public schools, and he proposed a set of four main goals:

> Beginning with narrowly academic and religious goals in the seventeenth century, vocational and social goals were added in the eighteenth and nineteenth centuries, and goals of personal or self-realization in the twentieth.[8]

Only the religious goals have fallen by the wayside, a necessity as the nation wove itself together from disparate colonies founded most often by individual religious denominations. The other four—academic, social, vocational, and personal—have remained, honored at least in commencement speech rhetoric, if not in daily practice.

We don't need to say much about the place of the academic goals of schooling. That seems to be all we ever hear about. When your local newspaper announces that your state has adopted new, world-class standards, do you think for even a second that these are standards of personal fulfillment or social involvement? Neither do we.

But what of the other three kinds of goals—social, vocational, and personal? All of us can name some class or program or activity in our own schooling that was designed to help meet one of these three kinds of aims, and clearly, these goals still exist. But our obsessive focus on academic "achievement" (as measured by standardized test scores) has pushed the other kinds of goals ever further toward the back of the "schooling" bus, where they are largely overlooked and left out of our public discourse. Maybe as a plea for attention these troublemaker goals should start shooting spitballs at the U.S. Secretary of Education, who sits smugly in the driver's seat with his back turned toward some major responsibilities of schooling. What do the troublemakers have to lose? They've already been expelled from public consciousness.

What have we lost by pushing these nonacademic goals to the back of the bus, along with social studies, the arts, and physical education? Think about what those parents of third-graders we mentioned above wanted for their own children. They wanted qualities that we don't always associate with classrooms: self-confidence, compassion, empathy, even happiness. But these remain important parts of the purpose of schooling in our society.

John Dewey got many things right, but by twenty-first-century standards his prose was ponderous, even Victorian. And like most philosophers, he often dealt in large, abstract ideas. If you take the time to read *Democracy and Education*, you'll find yourself nodding your head frequently. Unfortunately, we're afraid it might be drowsiness rather than agreement that brings on the nodding. But Dewey has had many translators. One, historian Lawrence Cremin, whom we quoted above, translated Dewey's abstract definition of education (a "reconstruction or reorganization of experience") into "a way of saying that the aim of education is not merely to make citizens, or workers, or fathers, or mothers, but ultimately to make human beings who will live life to the fullest."[9]

And it's that final statement we want to explore further. No matter how we spell out the various goals of schooling, we must remember what those third-grade parents seemed to know implicitly: When all is said and done, schools are a very important way of helping to create the next generation of people. Families, religious bodies, and other social institutions also play important roles, of course, but in our society, schools are critical. After all, students spend more than 15,000 hours in school over their twelve or thirteen years in attendance.

The aim of making a fully rounded human being came up a couple of years ago in an article by Herb Childress, a writer who often takes a critical look at high schools. Childress was examining the high school curriculum and addressing the goals of schooling in general. He broached the question of the broad purpose of schooling this way:

> [L]et's ask ourselves why we have them doing all these crazy things. [He's referring to things like conjugating French verbs or solving quadratic equations.] When I think about what high school is for, I remember that John Ogbu, the educational anthropologist, wrote that, "whatever else education may be, from the standpoint of society it is a preparation of children for adult life as adults in their society conceive it."[10]

So how would Childress conceive the kind of person we would want our schools to produce? With more time for reflection than the third-grade parents we've mentioned, Childress listed desirable characteristics for graduates of his ideal high school, and his list isn't all that different from what the parents wanted. Here it is, with our brief comments appended. Graduates should:

- *Love to read.* Adults in our society are expected to be literate, and we've never known a child who didn't want to join what Frank Smith has dubbed "the literacy club."
- *Enjoy numbers.* Adults in our society need to keep track of things. Note that Childress doesn't say be proficient in algebra or learn to use differential equations, but enjoying and being comfortable with numbers will make all kinds of quantitative tasks easier.
- *Enjoy physical exertion and activity.* Adults value fitness, even if they don't always pursue it. Any such activity we provide for young people will pay lifelong dividends in health and wellness.
- *Have some well-developed outlet for their creative desires.* From visual arts to woodworking to making music to gardening, creativity is part of being human.
- *Know how to work in groups and know how to teach a skill to someone else.* Everything that makes our society function is the work of collections of people; the solitary genius is largely a myth, and survival for such loners is every bit as tenuous as that of a real "lone wolf." (Coyotes banished from the pack, for example, have a mortality rate four times higher than pack members.) We are a social species.
- *Be brave and take risks.* Everyone needs to learn to fail and get up and try again. Schools should be safe environments where children can learn how.
- *Understand and take an interest in their community.* This includes everything from the local environment to local government to, yes, the local schools. Our rate of civic engagement may be low, but what is your school doing to improve it?
- *Be compassionate and care about people they don't know.* This is part of being a member of a social species. Failures are a part of adult life, and everyone needs and deserves support and understanding in coming back from them.[11]

There's a lot of academic *and* nonacademic learning going on in the ideal high school as Childress envisions it. His list provides a pretty good template for a successful adulthood in our society, though he hastens to add that he rarely encounters adults who exhibit all these characteristics. Moreover, it's a list of high—perhaps we should say world-class—standards, which he acknowledges he sometimes "fails to live up to." As do we.

But there is much on Childress's list that is simply not addressed in our schools, and under the regime of test-driven accountability, that list of untouched subjects only grows longer. Steven Wolk addressed just that question in an article aptly titled, "Why Go to School?"[12] What don't the schools teach that they really ought to if their goal is to help us produce the next generation of adults?

Wolk was set on this quest when he counted some four hundred worksheets that his second-grader brought home during the course of a school year. What were these low-level drills teaching his son? Not active learning or democratic citizenship. When professor dad was granted permission to substitute some real journal writing at home—a poem, a story, a letter—for the weekly spelling worksheets, his son resisted. He told his father that he wanted his homework to be "real school." He wanted to fill in blanks.

This disturbed Wolk and set him exploring the notion that our schools are unwittingly pursuing "schooling for anticitizenship." Despite what our school mission statements say, "we, the people," don't enable teachers to devote very much time to developing engaged citizens. Because we have decided to judge the success of our schools almost exclusively by test-based academic standards, teachers have scant time available to prepare our children to be well-rounded adults or engaged citizens. We have made a choice—even if it wasn't a conscious one—to push the historical purposes of public education off the stage. "Why are there no blazing headlines," Wolk asks, "condemning our schools for failing to prepare an educated and active citizenry?"[13] Consider this in light of Deborah Meier's call for us to provide "schooling for ruling." Maybe it would be more realistic to say we mostly provide schooling for "rule following"?

Among the things schools in this test-driven era aren't able to spend enough time on, Wolk numbers these (again with our comments following):

- *Self.* Who am I? Where did I come from? What makes me tick?
- *Love of learning.* This involves passion, and passion develops from human interaction. It can't be spoon-fed by means of a list of state standards.
- *Caring and empathy.* We often dismiss these as touchy-feely, but they grease the wheels of social interaction. Our society would be a harsh one without them.
- *Environmental literacy.* This topic grows more important with each generation.
- *Multicultural community.* This needs to mean more than tacos on Tuesdays.

- *Social responsibility.* A democracy is not just about rights; it's also about responsibilities.
- *Peace and nonviolence.* Citizens of any political persuasion ought to be able to support "peace" as a goal, even if it continues to elude our grasp.
- *Media literacy.* American children spend more time with the media than they do in school.[14] Nuff said?
- *Global awareness.* We hear lots about "globalism," but where education is concerned, it usually refers to comparisons of test scores. It shouldn't.
- *Creativity and imagination.* More than just art and aesthetics, creativity is about innovative thinking in any area.
- *Money, family, food, and happiness.* Not many things are more important than these four, and not much is said about them in schools after the early years.

IT STILL TAKES A VILLAGE

So now comes the hardest part. We said writing about the purposes of schooling wasn't going to be easy, and it hasn't been. But dealing with how a democratic society goes about settling on those purposes and the kind of support these purposes will require is even harder. For one thing, we often forget that the *education system* is far broader than the *school system*, for it includes the best efforts of families, religious institutions, preschools, sports leagues, service groups, and, yes, those universal electronic educators, television and the Internet. So if the purpose of *schooling* is to help bring the next generation of citizens into being, then all of those other institutions, as part of the total *education* system, also have a role to play. And they are every bit as accountable for that role as the schools are.

Keeping all of these players informed is really the purpose of our multiple accountability systems. That's what the proposals that we outlined in the preceding chapter, put forth by Ken Jones and by Richard Rothstein and his colleagues, aim to do. But if we're to keep tabs on our schools without having the whole exercise degenerate into a set of box scores where we track which school or district is in first place, or which state has the highest average NAEP scores, or even which nation is the top scorer on the Umpteenth International Mathematics and Science Study, we also need a way to get these players—call them the constituencies of schooling or call them the component parts of our society—engaged in the decisions we make about schooling.

While making decisions about schooling has always been the traditional role of school boards, we now have more students in public schools than ever before and fewer school boards. Rothstein and his colleagues offer some numbers: "In the mid-20th century, there were half a million school board members in the country."[15] That was for a nation of about 150 million people. Today, after major school consolidation, we have about 100,000 school board members, but they now serve some three hundred million people. The distance between board members and those they represent has grown dramatically. How many members of your local school board can you name? We can't name all of ours either. Gotcha questions like this one remind us of those items on standardized tests that only the "best" students are supposed to get right—they don't provide much useful information.

The important questions for everyone to answer—from parents to employers to retired folks—are these:

- What are the purposes of the public schools?
- How effective are the public schools in achieving those purposes?
- What changes are necessary to make the public schools as effective as we want them to be?[16]

And these were the very questions that Phi Delta Kappa, the National PTA, and the Center on Education Policy addressed in those twenty-eight public forums that we alluded to in a note in the previous chapter. Much was learned at these forums, whose participants were broadly representative of the communities where they were held. According to the organizers, the most successful ones were those that focused on districts. Why? Jack Jennings of the Center on Education Policy, one of the sponsors of the entire project, believes that the face-to-face contact at such events is crucial to building much-needed trust among the broad constituencies of the schools.[17]

One way to build that trust is to ensure that participation is as broad as possible. This means educators and those directly associated with schools should be participants in, but should not dominate, forum activities. Indeed, getting people without direct involvement in the schools to attend proved to be one of the hardest parts of the effort. Here's Jennings on that score:

> Getting members of society who are not associated with the public schools to attend these local forums has been one of the hardest aims to achieve. The local organizers have frequently spent hours trying to entice and cajole these people to come to the meeting, often with modest success. However, the most successful forums have been the ones in which all points of view were represented and educators were not in the majority.[18]

Paradoxically, the difficulty the organizers experienced in getting broad representation at the forums testifies to the need for such gatherings. Jennings reports on the mutual mistrust between many members of the public and those who work in the public schools: Educators seem to fear they will be attacked and that "outsiders" don't understand their work; noneducators seem to fear that they will be manipulated into blindly supporting the schools—and increasing funding. There may be historical reasons for such feelings, but there is no reason not to work to overcome them. If "it takes a village" to rear a child successfully, the village has to show up, make its collective views known, and work together to provide for the needs of its children—its next generation of adults.[19]

THE KIND OF SCHOOLS WE NEED

Throughout this book we've questioned the usefulness of standardized testing, which has become our society's preferred way of deciding whether or not our schools and students are succeeding. We've done that by challenging some of the basic assumptions of standardized tests that people rarely think about because the tests have become so commonplace. We wanted to help you understand that the tool chosen to tell us about our schools cannot do what we ask of it. Using test scores to pick winners and losers—whether states, districts, schools, or individuals—is misguided at best and truly harmful at worst.

Obviously, we hope our efforts ultimately help everyone do a better job of judging our public schools so that we can all work to improve the performance of those schools and the educators and students in them. We undertook this task, not with the goal of having our nation win some imagined "international Olympics of test-taking"—that would be to allow the tail of testing to keep wagging the dog of learning—but with an eye to enabling our schools to better fulfill the purposes they were created for. And those purposes, as John Goodlad and others have reminded us, are multiple. So too ought to be the expected outcomes of our schools.

But isn't that antidemocratic? Doesn't expecting a range of outcomes of schooling run counter to all our notions of equity? Just the reverse. What could be more inequitable than expecting everyone to learn the same things, to the same level of competence, in the same amount of time? When it's spelled out so baldly, that's plainly a stupid idea. What's even sillier, it seems, is that some of those who argue in favor of such expectations will turn right around and in the next breath tell you how much they value diversity and how important it is to the health of the nation. We have one word for such thinking, and the polite version is "Baloney!"

Now some of our leaders and many educators and their organizations have begun to recognize how unreasonable it is to ask everyone to get to the same place in the same amount of time. The solution they propose is to expand the time so everyone eventually gets to the destination. That's surely an improvement. But we ask you to think a little bit more about asking everyone to get to the same place—in whatever amount of time. Even if that were possible—and we don't think it is—is that what it means to be a successful adult in our society? When you look around at your friends and family members, are they all the same? How dreadful would it be if they were?

We prefer to fall in with Stanford University's Elliot Eisner, who wrote several years ago that "the kind of schools we need would not hold as an ideal that all students get to the same destinations at the same time. They would embrace the idea that good schools increase the variance in student performance and at the same time escalate the mean."[20] That's a professorial way of saying that we ought to become more different, rather than more alike, as we grow to physical and intellectual maturity. More different, yet we all grow.

Indeed, we believe it is central to creating a truly democratic system of schooling that we work to open a wide range of doors of opportunity and exploration for our children—and for ourselves if we were not so fortunate when we were young. We need to invite children in and lead them through these doors into all the areas of human life and learning—from art and anthropology to weather forecasting and zoology.

Of course, everyone will need to study some things in common. We see no problem there. We all need to read and write and cipher and know something of science and history and society. That's part of what it means to be a successful adult in our society. But as we introduce youngsters to these various paths of learning, we need to help them move along each path as far and as long as their aptitude and interest will take them. Sometimes we cajole. Sometimes we push a little. But we should never punish children for trying to find out who they are or for following the path that's right for them. Instead, we need to encourage them to explore all areas and develop those where their interests and aptitudes mesh.

Many teachers work to do just those things, and they do it within a system designed on an industrial model that always depended on having structured processes and machined parts that are as identical as possible. It's the hard work of such educators and the natural inclinations of their young charges that have kept us from creating a society of roboticized drones who do as they are told, show no initiative, and exhibit no spark of interest in learning. But by raising the bar of standards without regard for individual differences and by judging success primarily by scores on standardized tests, our policy environment has not been helpful.

We have enough faith in humankind to believe that an approach that follows student interest and develops student aptitudes will also take care of the pragmatic needs of society. If you know any engineers, you know that they didn't need to be pressured to learn the math and physics that enables them to create newer and better machines and structures. Engineers also know that they need to read and write functionally if they are to tell anyone who is not immediately present why and how the sewage system broke down. But some young engineers might choose to read only the minimal amount of Shakespeare required of them. Others might go so far in the other direction as to join a local amateur theater company. We heartily approve of both choices. Or ask any biologist or park ranger if his or her interest in living things derives from dad's promise of $5 for every A on a report card. If anything, as we pointed out in chapter 5, to the extent that the budding naturalist focused on earning the bribe, he or she was distracted from a naturally developing aptitude.

Now many people have multiple interests, and that is a good thing. Perhaps no more than 10 percent of the population actually *needs* to learn calculus for a career—and that's probably a high estimate. But everyone should be invited through the door and introduced to the attractions of the mathematics that leads to calculus and beyond. Young people need to explore many fields and life paths during their formative years if they are to find a best fit for themselves. If they don't do so then, when will they have a chance?

And if a child isn't interested in anything and just doesn't want to learn anything? What then? Then you have a problem that will probably require professional help beyond what we can reasonably expect of a classroom teacher who has responsibilities for all the rest of her charges. But coercion is *never* the right answer. And if that uninterested young person reaches the legal age to drop out and chooses to leave, what then? After doing everything we can to persuade such a person not to close the doors we've opened, we must reluctantly part ways. But we must never permanently close the doors to future learning. We need to design systems to help people of any age to embrace the learning they need and want. If not, we really aren't serious about endorsing the goal of lifelong learning. We're merely mouthing platitudes again.

But the breadth of developed talent and burgeoning interests that would emerge from a school that really did encourage the development of the widest possible range of student aptitudes would defy such simplistic measures as standardized tests. In our "best of all possible schools," judging how individuals are progressing toward their learning goals would be our most important evaluative task. And standardized tests, as we've tried to show throughout this book, are not very good at evaluating individual students fairly.

In this best of all possible schools the tests wouldn't even show up on students' radar screens, though they might play a small role in helping teachers

to target their instruction or in helping administrators to make some judgments. If your school system adopted a new math program, it might be useful
to test a sample of students to see whether the data showed any problems developing in a particular area. Say all the indicators in the fourth grade stayed
about the same except for a big drop in two-digit division. You still wouldn't
know for sure what was wrong, but at least you would have a place to start
looking—by talking to teachers and kids, by reexamining the textbooks and
supporting materials, and by observing some individual classes. This seems
to be a sensible use of a standardized test. And it would be inexpensive, for
you wouldn't need to test everyone; if the district is large enough, a representative sample would suffice.

How would you know how individual children are doing without a set
of test scores to tell you? We have contended throughout this book that the
scores don't really tell much that's useful. The simplest and best way to
learn how your child is progressing is to talk—with the teacher and with
your child. There are numerous informal opportunities for parents to do this,
of course, but among the best of the structured opportunities is the parent-
teacher conference.

We hope that students are included in these conferences, for it's important
that the leading actors know what part they're expected to play. When you look
at the triad of student-parent-teacher, you see in some ways a microcosm of a
democratic society. Some individuals have more official power than others—
parents in the home, teachers in the school. But real success in meeting the
goals of this minisociety depends on the success of the ordinary citizens (in
this analogy, the students) in pursuing their own purposes, arrived at mutu-
ally with parents and teachers. It is a joint effort, to be sure, but just as the
real strength of a democracy comes from the people, not the elected leaders,
so the real strength of a learning community comes not from state or national
standards but from the students' pursuit of their own learning goals.

But even if your school doesn't include students or doesn't make time for
more than a single conference each year, you can always ask to meet with
your child's teacher. We predict that you will be surprised by how willing
teachers are to do this. When you do, one of your purposes can be to learn
as much as you can about how the school uses (or doesn't use) the scores on
standardized tests. We've suggested a few questions (see "Some Test-Related
Questions to Share with Your Child's Teacher") that you might want to ask
your child's teacher at such a conference, but you'll surely have more and
some will be specific to your child's needs. And we predict that you'll learn
a great deal, about the tests, about their value or lack of it to the teachers,
but also about any other ways the teacher employs to keep track of student
progress.

SOME TEST-RELATED QUESTIONS TO SHARE WITH YOUR CHILD'S TEACHER

If you're reading this book, assessment and its uses are important topics to you, so when you have the chance to attend a parent-teacher conference, you have some homework to do beforehand. Be prepared to ask some questions about assessment and evaluation that can be important for you and your child. Teachers reading this book probably already expect to encounter a few such questions as well.

Of course, parents and teachers have many things other than assessment to talk about, and opening lines of communication in all the areas that are important to a child's education will pay dividends all year long. For example, you as a parent might need some additional explanation about the teacher's homework policy that was explained in the information that came home on the first day. Or you might want to know more about a teacher's discipline policies and how she might handle a particular situation. And don't forget that your child's teacher will welcome any information you consider important about your child and his or her learning history and behavior, both in school and out. Think about these things and be ready to offer information that you think the teacher might need to know.

Because we're focusing on assessment and evaluation, we're going to present just a handful of related questions aimed to improve the learning your child will do during the year and justifying the time, energy, and resources expended on assessment each year. But, to our teacher readers, forewarned is forearmed: it won't be easy to get some of the information that these questions ask for, though you might like to have it. Recall the difficulty Phil had in finding out simply how much time was devoted to the ITSTEP+ testing in Indiana (See Notes, chapter 2, note 7). What's more, Phil doesn't work in the school system and so didn't have to go outside of channels or over anyone's head to find the information. Teachers don't have that luxury and are constrained by their job role and by the traditions of secrecy surrounding all sorts of test-related information. So, parents, if you and your child's teacher believe that having a raw score (the number of items correct) or knowing which particular items a child missed could be useful, you can offer to help. It won't be easy for you as a parent to acquire some of this information either, but if you join forces with a few other parents from your child's class or school, you'll find that there is strength in numbers and that persistence pays off.

Now for the questions:

- Can you review for me, please, the standards being taught and tested?
- How would you say the textbooks you use match up to the standards?
- What tests will be administered? and when?
- How long has this test been used here?
- What is the purpose of such tests? (Don't accept "it's a state requirement" as an answer.)
- What use is made of the tests by the school or the district or the state?
- What is the class average (i.e., mean), and what is the range of scores?
- How do the test scores inform you as a teacher? What do they tell you about my child? How do you use the scores day-to-day? (These may be the most important questions of all.)
- How does the test help me as a parent to work with my child?
- Do you have the raw scores for my child? Percentile rankings and scaled scores can be confusing.
- Can you show me the particular items my child missed? If I want to help my child improve, I need to know where to start.
- When you observe my child in class, do you see his or her performance as consistent with the test scores?

These kinds of personal interactions amount to an alternative reporting system: Parents can learn all sorts of information that is particular to their child and his or her performance, interests, and goals; teachers can learn a great deal about their students' families, their views on education, and their hopes for their children. In short, both parties will learn things they can understand, need to know, and can do something with. This kind of person-to-person accountability beats a set of test scores any day.

Both school- and district-level accountability are important, as well, for they serve the information needs of society and so of all citizens. But they are not what parents and teachers care most about, nor are they what gives teachers the most useful information. For the higher-level accountability, we refer you to the accountability plans proposed by Richard Rothstein and Ken Jones and outlined in chapter 10. But parents and teachers need information that is particular to each child, and much of it they will need to develop themselves, in conjunction with individual learners. Thus a relationship of trust among teachers and parents and students is critical. Remember, if an ideal classroom is a learning community, that community includes not just a teacher and students; it includes parents as well.

You've stayed with us for a long time, and we thank you. Now, whether you're an educator, a parent, or perhaps both, it's time to move beyond the book.

If you're a parent, maybe your child has a teacher who has already reached out to the parents of her students. All sorts of mechanisms are available to teachers, ranging from a parent classroom handbook to phone calls and from e-mails and classroom blogs to invitations to parents to visit and volunteer to help in the classroom.[21] If your child's teacher has done any of these, count yourself lucky. But if not, when you put down this book, pick up the phone or send an e-mail to your child's teacher. It's less important that you have urgent information to share than that you open the lines of communication. Once you've done that, introduce her to the ideas in this book. If you're a teacher, put down the book and get in touch with the parents of your students. At the very least you'll give yourself the opportunity to learn a great deal more about your students. But whether you reach out from the school to the home or from the home to the school, either way, you will be taking the first step in building a relationship that will yield far more for the children we care about than any standardized test could ever do.

But don't stop there. Look back at the questions we listed in the Introduction. Then read some of the sources we cited in the subsequent chapters as we explored those questions and bring your own questions to your PTA meetings or to your school board meetings or, if you're a teacher, to your staff meetings. The original purpose of our schools was to prepare citizens who were capable of governing themselves. Let's show by our actions just how successful those schools have been.

A Resource Guide

When citizens have a problem with a public activity or service, the piece of advice likely to be offered is to write your elected representatives. That's not bad advice, and in fact it's necessary that many people chime in and make their views known. You elected these folks. You put them in office. They work for you, whether they're school board members, state representatives, or U.S. senators. But while such formal communication may be necessary—and we encourage it—it's not sufficient, especially when the clock is ticking. And where the education of a child is concerned, there just isn't any time to spare waiting for our elected leaders to see the light and act. We all know from experience that the wait can be years in length.

So what to do? By all means communicate with your elected representatives, and that includes everything from a formal letter to an e-mail or to a Saturday morning conversation with Joe, the school board chairman, while both of you are visiting the farmers' market. Then, too, every politician at every level—probably nearly every school board member—has a web page with information on ways to make contact. We don't think you need any more help pursuing this strategy. You know your local situation better than we ever could. As to chance meetings in the supermarket, just keep your eyes peeled.

But that's not all that you should do in the way of working politically. Grassroots movements have always surprised elected leaders in their power and their persistence, and today's digital magic makes them all the more potent as a force for change. The 2008 presidential election and Barack Obama's successful Internet fund-raising strategy make that clear. How about a flash mob that appears at the school board meeting after the state test scores are released and asks some of the questions we suggested that parents ask their children's teachers? Okay, maybe not.

If that's too radical, here's a short list of interesting sites on the web that you can explore and perhaps lend your support to. People across the country are concerned that all those tests used for accountability are having negative impacts on the next generation of Americans. Here are just a few sites where you can find some useful information and make contact with some interesting people. You might also have a bit of fun along the way. But don't forget to make use of old-fashioned networking, too. An unplanned discussion over the back fence or behind the backstop at the little league field can have every bit as much impact as an e-mail to a school board member or state representative. Maybe more. Now the list.

RESEARCH CENTERS

ERIC Clearinghouse on Assessment and Evaluation. This is the gateway to the federal site on education research that deals with assessment and evaluation. Be forewarned, though, that many of the entries are highly academic. http://ericae.net

The Center for the Study of Testing, Evaluation, and Educational Policy. Housed at Boston College for nearly three decades, the Center offers resources related to policy and practice in testing and evaluation. Again, it is largely an academic site. www.bc.edu/research/csteep

The National Center for Research on Evaluation, Standards, and Student Testing. This site offers the kind of monographs, papers, and reports to be expected from a university-based site. However, it also has special features for parents and for teachers, and it offers an "Ask the Expert" link. Try it. www.cse.ucla.edu

The Center on Education Policy. The CEP is an independent, national policy research center that advocates for better public schools. We've cited their work more than once in this book. Among the featured headings you'll find are testing, state testing data, No Child Left Behind, and high school exit exams. www.cep-dc.org

ORGANIZATIONS

The National Center for Fair and Open Testing (FairTest). Known as FairTest, this organization works to end the misuses and repair the flaws of standardized testing and to ensure that evaluation of students, teachers and schools is fair, open, valid, and educationally beneficial. It offers information on testing at all levels as well as advice on media relations. The organization also founded the Assessment Reform Network (ARN) and maintains a list of ARN state coordinators. www.fairtest.org

George Lucas Educational Foundation. The Lucas site offers an array of services and is home to a number of blogs. Under the "comprehensive assessment" link, there is information on authentic assessment and assessment for understanding as well as a complete library on assessment. The site also features useful and challenging questions that deal with real-life examples. www.edutopia.org

Public Broadcasting Service. Search on "standardized testing," and you'll find links to a number of John Merrow's reports that deal with issues surrounding testing, as well as interviews with James Popham and George Madaus and a *Frontline* feature titled "Testing Our Schools: A Guide for Parents," which is a reasonably balanced presentation of background information on tests and testing. If you're a teacher, the interactive site for teachers is worth a visit as well. www.pbs.org

Bolder, Broader Approach to Education. This campaign for a broader definition of schooling features an accountability page, which was a response to the 2006 effort to reauthorize No Child Left Behind. The central message is that "school improvement, to be fully effective, must be complemented by a broader definition of schooling [than the one taken by NCLB] and by improvements in the social and economic circumstances of disadvantaged youth." www.boldapproach.org

Rethinking Schools. This site is maintained by progressive educators, for progressive educators. Brought to you by the same people who publish the newspaper *Rethinking Schools*, the site features occasional articles on testing-related issues. www.rethinkingschools.org

The Forum on Educational Accountability. The Forum promotes positive changes in No Child Left Behind and other federal laws and policies. Among the changes it seeks is a call for multiple accountability measures at all levels, including writing samples, tasks, projects, and performances. www.edaccountability.org

Project Appleseed. Designed for parents of students who qualify for Title I funding, Project Appleseed offers much information that is useful to any and all parents. This link is to an online brochure on what standardized tests are, what they can do, and what they can't do. www.projectappleseed.org/standardtest.html

Time Out from Testing. This organization is a New York State organization of educators, parents, businesspeople, and civil rights advocates that is committed to taking a "time out" from excessive and inappropriate high-stakes testing. It is affiliated with www.performanceassessment.org. Both offer research reports and information on activism. www.timeoutfromtesting.org

The California Coalition for Authentic Reform in Education (Cal-Care). This organization seeks to organize resistance to mandated high-stakes testing. It encourages parents to "opt out" of the tests, which state law allows in California and many other states. www.calcare.org

PERSONAL SITES

Alfie Kohn writes and speaks widely on topics in education, behavior, and parenting. His site features a "special issue" on "standards and testing," where you'll find practical strategies to oppose the misuse of tests, links to other individuals and organizations that oppose testing, and some sample letters to superintendents and others. www.alfiekohn.org

Susan Ohanian is a teacher and writer who founded her website in 2003 to resist No Child Left Behind, and, along with Alfie Kohn's site, it is among the best personal sites. In the tradition of muckrakers of the past, Ohanian highlights outrageous stories of testing gone wrong and its impact on people, large and small. She also provides a great many links to other groups, and don't miss her satiric entries in "The Eggplant" or the delightful but depressing "Stupid Test Items." www.susanohanian.org

Notes

INTRODUCTION

1. Peter Wood, "How Our Culture Keeps Students Out of Science," *Chronicle of Higher Education*, 8 August 2008.

2. Henry Braun and Robert Mislevy, "Intuitive Test Theory," *Phi Delta Kappan*, March 2005, pp. 489–97.

3. Sarah Morin, "Funding the Only Clear Difference for State Superintendent Candidates," *Bloomington Herald-Times*, 1 October 2008.

4. Don't let terms such as *psychometrics* or *psychometrician* put you off. These are just fancy words for "mental measurement" and "those who conduct and study that measurement." We'll devote some space to definitions of other terms below.

5. "Standards for Educational and Psychological Testing," 1999, is available for a fee at http://www.apa.org/science/programs/testing/standards.aspx.

CHAPTER 1

1. *A Blueprint for Education Reform: The Reauthorization of the Elementary and Secondary Education Act* (Washington, DC: U.S. Department of Education, 2010).

2. Parts of this chapter appeared in Phillip Harris and Bruce Smith, "The Purpose Is the Point," *Education Week*, 12 May 2010, pp. 32–34.

3. Diane Ravitch, *The Death and Life of the Great American School System* (New York: Basic Books, 2010), p. 95.

4. Ibid., p. 230.

5. Ibid., pp. 227–28.

6. Gerald W. Bracey, "Nine Myths about U.S. Public Schools," Huffington Post, 25 September 2009.

7. Gerald W. Bracey, "Test Scores and Economic Competitiveness," *Phi Delta Kappan*, March 2007, pp. 554–57; "The 15th Bracey Report on the Condition of Education," *Phi Delta Kappan*, October 2005, pp. 138–53; "Put Out over PISA," *Phi Delta Kappan*, June 2005, pp. 797–98. See also appropriate sections of Bracey's books, *Setting the Record Straight* (Portsmouth, NH: Heinemann, 2004); and *On the Death of Childhood and the Destruction of Public Schools* (Portsmouth, NH; Heinemann, 2003).

8. Cited in Bracey, "Test Scores and Economic Competitiveness," p. 554.

9. W. Norton Grubb, "Dynamic Inequality and Intervention: Lessons from a Small Country," *Phi Delta Kappan*, October 2007, p. 113.

10. TIMSS Video Mathematics Research Group, "Understanding and Improving Mathematics Teaching: Highlights from the TIMSS 1999 Video Study," *Phi Delta Kappan*, June 2003, pp. 768–75.

CHAPTER 2

1. Definitions of "sampling error" and some other terms that might be unfamiliar can be found in "Say What?: An Abbreviated Glossary," beginning on page 187.

2. These "resources" are intended to help teachers, and so the classroom assessment items are not official candidates for inclusion in the state test, but their similarity in form is clear.

3. Weldon F. Zenger and Sharon K. Zenger, "Why Teach Certain Materials at Specific Grade Levels?" *Phi Delta Kappan*, November 2002, p. 212.

4. Daniel Koretz, *Measuring Up: What Educational Testing Really Tells Us* (Cambridge, MA: Harvard University Press, 2008), p. 21.

5. W. James Popham, *Transformative Assessment* (Alexandria, VA: Association for Supervision and Curriculum Development, 2008), pp. 124–25.

6. Alfie Kohn, *The Case against Standardized Testing: Raising the Scores, Ruining the Schools* (Portsmouth, NH: Heinemann, 2000), p. 13.

7. The numbers we cite come from the state department, and it wasn't all that easy to get them. Curiously, a principal we consulted didn't have any record of the data, nor did the local district office. Indeed, it took several phone calls to the state department before we got an answer. And the link to the online manual for administering the test was "inoperative" on the days we checked it.

CHAPTER 3

1. Richard Rothstein, *The Way We Were? The Myths and Realities of America's Student Achievement* (New York: Century Foundation, 1998), p. 3.

2. Signs in the rhetoric of the "blueprint" suggest that the Obama administration hopes to spur the development of tests that are more comprehensive than the ones common under No Child Left Behind. But skepticism runs high, as Nel Noddings

says, "We've just gone test crazy." Catherine Gewertz, "Race to the Top Rules Aim to Spur Shifts in Testing," *Education Week*, 8 April 2010.

3. Rochelle Gutiérrez, Jennifer Bay-Williams, and Timothy D. Kanold, "Equity," *NCTM News Bulletin*, October 2008, p. 5. The work cited is Rochelle Gutiérrez, "A 'Gap-Gazing' Fetish in Mathematics Education? Problematizing Research on the Achievement Gap," *Journal for Research in Mathematics Education*, July 2008, pp. 357–64.

4. Daniel Koretz, *Measuring Up* (Cambridge, MA: Harvard University Press, 2008), p. 9.

5. Gerald W. Bracey, *Setting the Record Straight*, 2nd ed. (Portsmouth, NH: Heinemann, 2004), p. 32.

6. Alfie Kohn, *The Case against Standardized Testing: Raising the Scores, Ruining the Schools* (Portsmouth, NH: Heinemann, 2000), p. 10. Kohn provides interested readers with citations to these two studies.

7. Koretz, p. 9.

8. Stephen Jay Gould, *The Mismeasure of Man* (1981; rev. and ex., New York: Norton, 1996), p. 50.

9. Robin McKie, "Americans Shrinking as Junk Food Takes Its Toll," 4 April 2004, http://www.guardian.co.uk/world/2004/apr/04/usa.

10. Huang Dantong et al., "Exercise Plus Milk Increases Height of Japanese Children by 12 cm," *Guangzhou Daily* (English Special), 15 August 2008. gzdaily.dayoo .com/html/2008-08/15/content_290508.htm.

11. Thomas Toch, "Test Results and Drive-By Evaluations," *Education Week*, 5 March 2008.

12. W. James Popham, *Transformative Assessment* (Alexandria, VA: Association for Supervision and Curriculum Development, 2008), p. 124.

13. W. James Popham, *Truth in Testing* (Alexandria, VA: Association for Supervision and Curriculum Development, 2001), p. 43.

14. Ibid., p. 48.

15. Toch, op. cit.

16. Koretz, p. 326.

CHAPTER 4

1. Good luck typing the URL for "CLEP: Promoting Academic Success in Higher Education." We're not even including it here because it's four lines of gibberish. The best way to find the document we're referring to here is to google the title.

2. Richard Rothstein, *The Way We Were? The Myths and Realities of America's Student Achievement* (New York: Century Foundation Press, 1998), p. 72.

3. Richard Rothstein, Rebecca Jacobsen, and Tamara Wilder, *Grading Education: Getting Accountability Right* (Washington, DC, and New York: Economic Policy Institute and Teachers College Press, 2008), p. 63. The report quoted is: Susan Cooper

Loomis and Mary Lyn Bourque, eds., *National Assessment of Educational Progress Achievement Levels, 1992–1998 for Mathematics* (Washington, DC: National Assessment Governing Board, July 2001). A similar statement appears in a companion report on NAEP levels for writing.

4. James Pellegrino, "Should NAEP Performance Standards Be Used for Setting Standards for State Assessments?" *Phi Delta Kappan,* March 2007, p. 540.

5. Quoted in Anne Lewis, "Assessing Student Achievement: Search for Validity and Balance," CSE Technical Report 481, Los Angeles, June 1998, p. 26.

6. Gerald W. Bracey, *Setting the Record Straight* (Portsmouth, NH: Heinemann, 2004), p. 73. Bracey gives references for the four studies cited in his text, but for those who wish to follow up, here they are, along with a couple of others: *Educational Achievement Standards: NAGB's Approach Yields Misleading Interpretations* (Washington, DC: General Accounting Office, 1993); *Assessment in Transition: Monitoring the Nation's Educational Progress* (Mountain View, CA: National Academy of Education, 1997); *Setting Performance Standards for Student Achievement: A Report of the National Academy of Education Panel on the Evaluation of the NAEP Trial State Assessment: An Evaluation of the 1992 Achievement Levels* (Stanford, CA: National Academy of Education, 1993); *Grading the Nation's Report Card: Evaluating NAEP and Transforming the Assessment of Educational Progress* (Washington, DC: National Academy of Sciences, 1999); and Robert L. Linn, "Standards-Based Accountability: Ten Suggestions," CRESST, University of California, Los Angeles, 1998.

7. Nicole Brooks, "ISTEP Scores Rise This Year at MCCSC," *Bloomington Herald-Times,* 4 December 2008.

8. Ibid.

9. Theodore M. Porter, *Trust in Numbers: The Pursuit of Objectivity in Science and Public Life* (Princeton, NJ: Princeton University Press, 1996).

10. Nikolas Rose, "Governing Medical Judgment: The Logics of Objectivity: Searching for Gold Standards." Because the URL is so long, the best way to find this document is simply to google the title.

CHAPTER 5

1. Alfie Kohn, *Punished by Rewards: The Trouble with Gold Stars, Incentive Plans, A's, Praise, and Other Bribes* (1993; New York: Houghton Mifflin, 1999).

2. Alfie Kohn, *The Case against Standardized Testing: Raising the Scores, Ruining the Schools* (Portsmouth, NH: Heinemann, 2000).

3. Alex Duran, "Factors to Consider When Evaluating School Accountability Results," *Journal of Law and Education,* January 2005, p. 13.

4. Heinrich Mintrop, "The Limits of Sanctions in Low-Performing Schools: A Study of Maryland and Kentucky Schools on Probation," *Education Policy Analysis Archives,* January 2003, http://epaa.asu.edu/epaa/v11n3.html.

5. Damien Betebenner, "Review of 'Feeling the Florida Heat? How Low-Performing Schools Respond to Voucher and Accountability Pressure,' by Cecelia Elena

Rouse et al., Urban Institute's National Center for Analysis of Longitudinal Data in Education Research, November 2007," Think Tank Review Project, Great Lakes Center for Education Research & Practice, January 2008.

6. We should say a word about a widespread misunderstanding of the language of behaviorism, the language of punishments and rewards. In casual conversation about children, we've all heard more than one parent remark that she chooses "positive reinforcement" for Johnny and doesn't like to resort to "negative reinforcement," which is presumably the heavy artillery of imposing a punishment. But this reflects the common confusion between negative reinforcement and punishment and between positive reinforcement and reward. It's worth a paragraph or two to set the record straight, though we don't expect to change popular usage of the terms. One of the most accessible explanations we know—both in being easily understood and widely available—is in Cesar Millan's *Be the Pack Leader* (Three Rivers Press, 2007). In a chapter titled "Discipline, Rewards, and Punishment," he passes on clinical psychologist Alice Clearman's explanation:

[T]here are two basic ways of changing all behavior—reinforcement and punishment. In human psychology, there is positive punishment and positive reinforcement, and there is negative punishment and negative reinforcement. Positive and negative work the same way that they do in simple math. If you add something, it's a positive. If you subtract something, it's a negative. Positive reinforcement means adding something I like to encourage me to repeat a behavior. If I give a seminar and receive a standing ovation, it reinforces my experience of giving the seminar, and I'll want to do it again. Negative reinforcement is often thought of as equivalent to punishment, but it is absolutely not punishment. Negative reinforcement is when you reinforce a behavior by removing something someone doesn't like. Dr. Clearman uses the example of taking aspirin for a headache. If she has a headache, takes an aspirin, and her headache goes away, she has successfully reinforced herself for taking aspirin. The aspirin removed the headache—the thing she didn't like (pp. 47–48).

The confusion surrounding these terms is why we're sticking to rewards (desirable) and punishments (undesirable). We're not worried about distinguishing between not having to take the final if you've earned an A on all the preceding tests (a negative reinforcement) and, say, earning actual cash for high grades and test scores (a positive reinforcement).

7. Antoinette Roth, chair, Mid-Atlantic Regional Advisory Committee, Report to the U.S. Department of Education, March 2005. To locate a pdf of this document, simply google the committee's title.

8. *Punished by Rewards*, chap. 4 and 5.

9. Edward L. Deci, R. Koestner, and Richard M. Ryan, "A Meta-analytic Review of Experiments Examining the Effects of Extrinsic Rewards on Intrinsic Motivation," *Psychological Bulletin*, vol. 125, 1999, pp. 627–68. For an annotated summary of this research, along with countervailing points of view, see "The Rewards Controversy," www.psych.rochester.edu/#141643.

10. Daniel T. Willingham, "Should Learning Be Its Own Reward?" *American Educator*, Winter 2007–2008, available on the website of the American Federation of Teachers, www.aft.org.

11. There have been a few recent efforts to try paying students directly for either test scores or grades, and New York City now has a number of incentive programs in a range of social services. See Jennifer Medina, "Schools Plan to Pay Cash for Marks," *New York Times*, 19 June 2007. In at least one case of direct payment for taking Advanced Placement tests, the early results, as we would have predicted, have not been what proponents hoped for. See Elissa Gootman, "Mixed Results on Paying City Students to Take Tests," *New York Times*, 19 August 2008. One finding from this effort in New York: more students took AP tests; fewer passed.

12. Sharon L. Nichols and David C. Berliner, *Collateral Damage: How High-Stakes Testing Corrupts America's Schools* (Cambridge, MA: Harvard Education Press, 2007), p. 18.

13. A recent example is a commentary by Marguerite Roza, Dan Goldhaber, and Paul T. Hill, "The Productivity Imperative," *Education Week*, 7 January 2009, pp. 48, 34. It's easy to endorse the idea that schools should be run efficiently, but the authors end up seeming to endorse achievement test scores as the measure of effectiveness.

14. On schools giving up letter grades, see, for example, T. S. Mills-Faraudo, "Schools Toss Out Letter Grades," *Oakland Tribune*, 14 September 2006; and M. Jon Dean, "Can We Get Beyond Letter Grades?" *Educational Leadership*, May 2006. On the more than 775 colleges that have gone "test optional," see the website of FairTest at www.fairtest.org.

15. Kohn, p. 182, quotes Deming and paraphrases Frederick Herzberg.

16. Donald B. Gratz, "Lessons from Denver: The Pay for Performance Pilot," *Phi Delta Kappan*, April 2005, pp. 579–80.

17. Ibid., p. 570. Gratz is quoting Wellford W. Wilms and Richard R. Chapleau, "The Illusion of Paying Teachers for Student Performance," *Education Week*, 3 November 1999, p. 48. For a good history of testing, see George Madaus, Michael Russell, and Jennifer Higgins, *The Paradoxes of High Stakes Testing* (Charlotte, NC: Information Age Publishing, 2009), chap. 5.

CHAPTER 6

1. Donald Campbell, "Assessing the Impact of Planned Social Change," in Gene Lyons, ed., *Social Research and Public Policies: The Dartmouth/OECD Conference* (Hanover, NH: Public Affairs Center, Dartmouth College, 1975).

2. Sharon L. Nichols and David C. Berliner, *Collateral Damage: How High-Stakes Testing Corrupts America's Schools* (Cambridge, MA: Harvard Education Press, 2007). Of course, they are not alone. See also M. Gail Jones, Brett Jones, and Tracy Hargrove, *The Unintended Consequences of High-Stakes Testing* (Lanham, MD: Rowman & Littlefield, 2003).

3. For many examples of a range of questionable behaviors by educators and students, see Nichols and Berliner, chap. 3.

4. Brian Jacob and Steven D. Levitt, "To Catch a Cheat," *Education Next*, Winter 2004. The probation policy required schools to post at least 15 percent of their students' scores above national norms or face the possibility of sanctions, leading ultimately to a reconstitution of the school. http://educationnext.org/tocatchacheat/.

5. Ibid.

6. Ibid.

7. Nichols and Berliner, p. 60.

8. See Jacquie McTaggart, "Why Some Teachers Cheat," 10 June 2008, at http://ednews.org/articles/26300/1/Why-Some-Teachers-Cheat/Page1.html; among the articles she quotes is Nanette Asimov and Todd Wallach, "The Teachers Who Cheat," *San Francisco Chronicle*, 13 May 2007. See also Joshua Benton and Holly K. Hacker, "Analysis Shows TAKS Cheating Rampant," *Dallas Morning News*, 3 June 2007. This last item was part of a two-year-long series of articles in *Dallas Morning News* that also included Joshua Benton, "TEA: Teacher Leaked Part of TAKS Test," *Dallas Morning News*, 13 July 2007, wherein the accused teacher admitted his actions and said he was just trying to help his school and was doing what everyone else did. The problems are nationwide. In Massachusetts, see Tracy Jan, "Cheating on MCAS Doubles," *Boston Globe*, 1 November 2007; in Georgia, see D. Aileen Dodd, "Gwinnett Teachers Accused of CRCT Cheating," *Atlanta Journal-Constitution*, 7 July 2008.

9. The Schools Matter website (schoolsmatter.blogspot.c#1463F4) provides a link to "Disappearing Dropouts," a November 2004 report by education reporter John Merrow, that provides details on how a school's total graduation class can decline while its dropout rate falls. For those interested in policy research supporting the idea that dropout rates (no matter how you calculate them!) go up when the stakes on tests are high, see John R. Warren, Krista N. Jenkins, and Rachael B. Kulik, "High School Exit Examinations and State-level Completion and GED Rates, 1975–2002," *Educational Evaluation and Policy Analysis*, vol. 28, 2006. (Google the title.) For research that debunks the notion that high school graduation tests improve achievement, see Eric Grodsky, John R. Warren, and Demetra Kalogrides, "State High School Exit Examinations and NAEP Long-Term Trends in Reading and Mathematics, 1971–2004," *Educational Policy*, 13 June 2008.

10. According to Anne Wheelock, an independent researcher working with Boston College, "Many schools that won awards increased their grade retention and dropout rates, which made it easier for them to raise school scores enough to win an award. This is true of four of the six 2002 'Compass' high schools named by the [Massachusetts] Department of Education. The state has no program to reduce dropout rates and no procedures to make sure school scores do not benefit from inappropriate practices or even from pushing kids out." Wheelock was quoted in "New Study Finds Rewarding Schools for MCAS Score Gains Produces Flawed Results, Encourages Inappropriate Practices," press release, www.fairtest.org, 27 June 2002. To see the

impact of a high-stakes policy on dropout data for a large urban district, especially with regard to its impact on minority students, see Linda M. McNeil et al., "Avoidable Losses: High Stakes Accountability and the Dropout Crisis," *Education Policy Analysis Archives*, January 2008, http://epaa.asu.edu/epaa/v16n3/. The study by researchers headquartered at Rice University found that 60 percent of African American students, 75 percent of Latino students, and 80 percent of ESL (English as a Second Language) students did not graduate within five years.

11. The matter of retention in grade versus what has been called "social promotion" requires a book-length treatment of its own, but for those interested in learning more, here's a good way to get started. Read Colleen Stump, "Repeating a Grade: The Pros and Cons," *GreatSchools*, April 2008, www.greatschools.net. This article is an excellent summary of the research on the impact of grade retention, and it is aimed at parents. Along the way, the author cites a 2003 position paper on the subject by the National Association of School Psychologists (www.nasp.org), which concluded, among other things:

- Academic achievement of kids who are retained is poorer than that of peers who are promoted.
- Achievement gains associated with retention fade within two to three years after the grade repeated.
- Kids who are identified as most behind are the ones "most likely harmed by retention."
- Retention often is associated with increased behavior problems.
- Grade retention has a negative impact on all areas of a child's achievement (reading, math, and language) and socioemotional adjustment (peer relationships, self-esteem, problem behaviors, and attendance).
- Students who are retained are more likely to drop out of school compared to students who were never retained. In fact, grade retention is one of the most powerful predictors of high school dropout.

Like the use of rewards and punishments, retaining students in grade, which seems logical, is most often counterproductive. And if you'd like to hit your local school board with a couple of counterintuitive ideas at once, try suggesting that both the rewards and punishments associated with standardized tests and the practice of retention in grade be consigned to the dustbin of history, where they clearly belong. Just make sure you've done your homework in advance and read, not just this book, but the books and papers we've cited. And be sure to know where the rear exit to the meeting hall is located in case you need to make a quick getaway.

12. Lawrence Mishel and Joydeep Roy, "Education Week's Graduation Rate Estimates Are 'Exceedingly Inaccurate,' Experts Say," Economic Policy Institute, June 2008, www.epi.org. This commentary carries links to the views of an impressive array of analysts.

13. "Executive Summary, Diplomas Count 2008: School to College," *Education Week*, 5 June 2008, www.edweek.org.

14. Nichols and Berliner, p. 75.

15. "Summary: Lessons from the Classroom Level about Federal and State Accountability in Rhode Island and Illinois," Center on Education Policy, Washington, DC, 6 February 2009, www.cep-dc.org.

16. The definitive studies of bubble kids in the United States have been conducted by Jennifer Booher-Jennings. See Jennifer Booher-Jennings, "Below the Bubble: 'Educational Triage' and the Texas Accountability System," *American Educational Research Journal*, vol. 42, 2005, pp. 231–68; and idem, "Rationing Education in an Era of Accountability," *Phi Delta Kappan*, June 2006, pp. 756–61. She attributes the use of the term *educational triage* to David Gillborn and Deborah Youdell, *Rational Education: Policy, Practice, Reform, and Equity* (Buckingham, UK: Open University Press, 2000).

17. "Summary: Lessons . . ." op. cit.

18. Nichols and Berliner (p. 122) cite journalist Jay Mathews's article "Let's Teach to the Test," *Washington Post*, 20 February 2006, p. A-1, as one place where the claim is made. But Mathews is not the first to raise the issue, and he is far from alone.

19. Nichols and Berliner, p. 124.

20. Ibid., p. 123. Nichols and Berliner are citing M. Gail Jones et al., "The Impact of High-Stakes Testing on Teachers and Students in North Carolina," *Phi Delta Kappan*, November 1999, p. 201. Jones and her colleagues are reporting on the ABCs accountability program in North Carolina in the late 1990s (pre-NCLB), which included monetary rewards for teachers as well as severe sanctions for schools that failed to meet test score goals.

21. "Elementary Schools Impacted More by NCLB and Illinois Accountability Than High Schools," press release, Center on Education Policy, Washington, DC, 22 December 2008.

22. Nichols and Berliner, p. 122.

CHAPTER 7

1. Adding science in 2008 to the federal roster of subjects to be tested changes its situation some. Exactly how, though, is not yet clear.

2. Stephen J. Dubner, "What Should Be Done about Standardized Tests? A Freakonomics Quorum," 20 December 2007, posting by Monty Neill. In addition to Neill, the quorum included contributions from James Popham, Robert Zemsky, Thomas Toch, and Gaston Caperton.

3. Jennifer McMurrer, *Instructional Time in Elementary Schools: A Closer Look at Specific Subjects* (Washington, DC: Center on Education Policy, February 2008). Available at www.cep-dc.org; search on the title.

4. Tara Parker-Pope, "The 3 R's? A Fourth Is Crucial, Too: Recess," *New York Times*, 2 February 2009. The original study was Romina M. Barros, Ellen J. Silver, and Ruth E. K. Stein, "School Recess and Good Classroom Behavior," *Pediatrics*, 1 February 2009. To find it, google the title.

5. "Strong Relationship between Kids' Academic Achievement and Fitness," 19 October 2004, reporting on studies conducted at the University of Illinois (www. news-medical.net/?id=5684); and Virginia R. Chomnitz et al., "Is There a Relationship between Physical Fitness and Academic Achievement? Positive Results from Public School Children in the Northeastern United States," *Journal of School Health*, 1 January 2009.

6. "No Time for Recess, No Need for Nap," FairTest, May 2004 (www.fairtest. org; search on "recess").

7. A brief history of modern testing in schools, roughly since the 1960s, can be found in W. James Popham, *The Truth about Testing* (Alexandria, VA: Association for Supervision and Curriculum Development, 2001), pp. 4–8.

8. For a good summary of the distinctions between authentic assessment and performance assessment, see Daniel Koretz, *Measuring Up: What Educational Testing Really Tells Us* (Cambridge, MA: Harvard University Press, 2008), pp. 59–63.

9. Pressure from these people, who control a great deal of funding, has not been without controversy, especially with regard to moving the standards into ever lower grade levels, and in the future, even into preschools. See Catherine Gewertz, "Both Value and Harm Seen in K–3 Common Core Standards," *Education Week*, 8 April 2010.

10. Sharon L. Nichols and David C. Berliner, *Collateral Damage: How High-Stakes Testing Corrupts America's Schools* (Cambridge, MA: Harvard Education Press, 2007), p. 5.

11. *Country School Examinations: Winter Term 1913*, collected by Jennie M. Kaufman, John J. Austin, ed. (Muskegon, MI: Research Concepts, 1970), n.p.

CHAPTER 8

1. The quotation in text is a summary of the conclusions of Clarence E. Ridley and Herbert A. Simon, *Measuring Municipal Activities* (Chicago: International City Managers' Association, 1938). It is taken from Richard Rothstein, Rebecca Jacobsen, and Tamara Wilder, *Grading Education: Getting Accountability Right* (New York: Teachers College Press, 2009), p. 75.

2. FairTest Fact Sheet, "SAT I: A Faulty Instrument for Predicting College Success," 20 August 2007, www.fairtest.org. Search on the title. The SAT I correlates with first-year college grades at just about 0.47 or 0.48; high school grades correlate at just over 0.50. To explain the differences in first-year grades, however, these correlations must be squared. Thus the SAT I comes in at 22 percent or 23 percent, while grades come in at a little over 26 percent. Together, you could do worse than think of them as explaining just under 30 percent of the difference in first-year college grades.

3. *What Is the Value of the Graduate Record Examination?* (Princeton, NJ: ETS, 2008).

4. Michael Winerip, "Standardized Tests Face a Crisis over Standards," *New York Times*, 22 March 2008.

5. Caroline M. Hoxby, "Conversion of a Standardized Test Skeptic," Hoover Institution, Stanford University, 1 June 2001. Google the title. Hoxby's figure is

somewhere between $2.50 and $5 per multiple-choice test, and though her figures are a few years older than the cost for essay scoring we've cited, she does build a lot of air into them. And remember, this is an entire test versus a single essay item.

6. Rothstein, Jacobsen, and Wilder, p. 7.

CHAPTER 9

1. Daniel Goleman, "75 Years Later, Study Still Tracking Geniuses," *New York Times*, 7 March 1995. This article actually cites 135 as the IQ cutoff that Terman used, but 140 is more commonly reported. In either case, those above the line fall roughly into the top 1 percent of the population.

2. Rebecca Coffey, "Things You Didn't Know about Genius," *Discover*, October 2008, p. 88; and "Child Prodigies," http://brainconnection.positscience.com/topics/?main=fa/child-prodigies.

3. David F. Lohman, "An Aptitude Perspective on Talent: Implications for Identification of Academically Gifted Students," *Journal for Gifted Education*, vol. 28, 2005, pp. 333–60. Lohman is primarily concerned with the selection of students for gifted programs, and he points out discrepancies between the students selected by means of scores on the ITBS and those selected by scores on the Cognitive Abilities Test (a reasoning/IQ test)—this despite the high correlation between the two tests of roughly 0.80.

4. Leonard L. Baird, "Do Grades and Tests Predict Adult Accomplishment?" *Research in Higher Education*, vol. 23, no. 1, 1985, pp. 3–85.

5. Ibid., p. 3. The quotation is from Baird's overall conclusion as expressed in the abstract to his study.

6. The College Board report mentioned by this researcher is *On Further Examination*, a 1977 report from a panel chaired by former U.S. Secretary of Labor Willard Wirtz that speculated on reasons for the decline in SAT scores between the mid-1960s and the late 1970s. The panel proposed explanations ranging from excessive television viewing to a decline in family values. Researchers generally discounted such explanations. Nevertheless, the report garnered many headlines in the late 1970s, and, though SAT scores were never intended to measure school performance, the report influenced discussions of school policies and was part of the backdrop for *A Nation at Risk*, the 1983 report of the National Commission on Excellence in Education.

7. Baird, p. 4.

8. Baird, p. 59.

9. Gerald W. Bracey, *Education Hell: Rhetoric vs. Reality* (Alexandria, VA: Educational Research Service, 2009), p. 73.

10. Nathan R. Kuncel and Sarah A. Hezlett, "Standardized Tests Predict Graduate Student Success," *Science*, 23 February 2007, pp. 1080–81.

11. "A Defence of Standardized Testing," *Inside Higher Education*, 23 February 2007 (www.insidehighered.com/news/2007/02/23/tests#Comments). This online article is essentially an interview with Nathan Kuncel, and FairTest's Bob Schaeffer is quoted briefly.

12. "ETS to Introduce Evaluation System for Critical Personal Attributes," ETS Press Release, 5 December 2008.

13. We're focusing on the "individual" cost of college admission tests such as the SAT, not the overall national cost. FairTest cited $150 million as the total of SAT fees in 2006, but Gerald Bracey cited the same figure in 1989 in "The $150 Million Redundancy," *Phi Delta Kappan*, May 1989, pp. 698–72, and we know that fees and numbers have risen in the intervening years. FairTest also cites a figure of $350 million for test prep. We believe both numbers underestimate the total cost in terms of time, test prep (whether formal or informal), and what amounts to national obsession.

14. Saul Geiser and Maria Veronica Santelices, "Validity of High-School Grades in Predicting Student Success beyond the Freshman Year," Center for Studies in Higher Education, Research & Occasional Paper Series: CSHE.6.07, University of California, Berkeley, June 2007.

15. FairTest tracks this figure closely at www.fairtest.org.

16. Schaeffer referred to this practice on NPR's *Frontline* a few years back. "Interview with Bob Schaeffer," *Frontline: Secrets of the SAT*, 1999, available at http://www.pbs.org/wgbh/pages/frontline/shows/sats/interviews/schaeffer.html.

17. Rebecca Zwick, *Fair Game?: The Use of Standardized Admissions Tests in Higher Education* (New York: Routledge/Falmer, 2002), p. 96.

18. "Standards for Educational and Psychological Testing," 1999, is available for a fee at www.apa.org/science/standards.html. A panel was appointed to revise these standards in September 2008.

CHAPTER 10

1. A little over a decade ago Phi Delta Kappa International, the Center on Education Policy, and the National PTA jointly sponsored a project designed to engage the public at the community level in discussions designed to build support for and give direction to the local public schools. Twenty-eight forums were held over the span of slightly more than a year. See Lowell C. Rose, "The Future of the Public Schools: A Public Discussion," *Phi Delta Kappan*, June 1997, pp. 765–68; John F. Jennings, "An Experiment in Democracy," *Phi Delta Kappan*, June 1997, pp. 769–71; and E. Arthur Stunard, "The Chicago Forum," *Phi Delta Kappan*, June 1997, pp. 774–76.

2. Andy Graham, "MCCSC Fails Test for Second Year in a Row," *Bloomington Herald-Times*, 16 April 2009, p. 1.

3. Frederick M. Hess, "The New Stupid: Limitations of Data-Driven Education Reform," *AEI Education Outlook*, January 2009, p. 1.

4. Ken Jones, "A Balanced School Accountability Model: An Alternative to High-Stakes Testing," *Phi Delta Kappan*, April 2004, pp. 584–90.

5. As this book went to press, a panel of leading pscyhometricians and education researchers issued a report that raised a yellow caution flag with regard to using student test scores to evaluate teachers. See Eva L. Baker et al., "Problems with the Use of Student Test Scores to Evaluate Teachers," Economic Policy Institute, Briefing Paper No. 278, August 27, 2010.

6. Ibid., p. 589.

7. Ibid., p. 585.

8. Richard Rothstein, Rebecca Jacobsen, and Tamara Wilder, *Grading Education: Getting Accountability Right* (Washington, DC, and New York: Economic Policy Institute and Teachers College Press, 2008).

9. By the way, this would still be true for schools even if the standardized tests used were impeccably designed and did pretty much everything their most ardent advocates claim. We need to wait years—sometimes decades—to see the eventual results of our schools' public service.

10. Rothstein, Jacobsen, and Wilder, p. 75.

11. Ibid., p. 73.

CHAPTER 11

1. Deborah Meier, "Democracy at Risk," *Educational Leadership*, May 2009, p. 45.

2. In chapter 11 of *Education Hell: Rhetoric vs. Reality* (Alexandria, VA: Educational Research Service, 2009), Gerald Bracey has gathered three separate essays that explore the place of education for democracy. The essays by Richard Gibboney and Deborah Meier explore the poisonous impact of poverty on our democracy and its institutions, while Nel Noddings looks at the essentially undemocratic nature of the push for "college for all."

3. The text of Franklin's proposal is available in a number of places, including www.archives.upenn.edu/primdocs/1749proposals.html.

4. Lawrence A. Cremin, *American Education: The National Experience, 1783–1876* (New York: Harper & Row, 1980), p. 2. Note that Cremin, like Franklin and Jefferson, refers to a "republic," which is technically correct for, even today, the U.S. government is a republic, not a true democracy. It was even less a democracy when Franklin and Jefferson were busy creating it.

5. Jennings L. Wagoner Jr., *Jefferson and Education* (Monticello: Thomas Jefferson Foundation, Monticello Monograph Series, 2004), p. 128.

6. The Rockfish Gap Report was a report of a commission established to select a site for the University of Virginia. The easiest way to find it today is to google the title, which will take you to the report itself at the University of Virginia libraries.

7. Larry Cuban, "Why Bad Reforms Won't Give Us Good Schools," *American Prospect*, 1 January 2009.

8. John I. Goodlad, *What Schools Are For* (Bloomington, IN: Phi Delta Kappa Educational Foundation, 1979), p. 58. If education has an elder statesman today, that person is no doubt John Goodlad.

9. Lawrence A. Cremin, *The Transformation of the School* (New York: Alfred A. Knopf, 1961), pp. 122–23.

10. Herb Childress, "A Subtractive Education," *Phi Delta Kappan*, October 2006, p. 106.

11. Ibid., pp. 106–7. The complete article is available free to members of Phi Delta Kappa at www.pdkintl.org; search the archives. Nonmembers may purchase a copy for a small fee.

12. Steven Wolk, "Why Go to School?" *Phi Delta Kappan*, May 2007, pp. 648–58.

13. Ibid., p. 651.

14. Ibid., p. 655, citing Henry K. Kaiser Family Foundation, "Generation M: Media in the Lives of 8–18 Year-Olds," March 2005. Search at www.kff.org, or google the title.

15. Richard Rothstein, Rebecca Jacobsen, and Tamara Wilder, *Grading Education: Getting Accountability Right* (Washington, DC, and New York: Economic Policy Institute and Teachers College Press, 2008), p. 121.

16. Lowell C. Rose and Dana Rapp, "The Future of the Public Schools: A Public Discussion," *Phi Delta Kappan*, June 1997, pp. 765–68.

17. John F. (Jack) Jennings, "An Experiment in Democracy," *Phi Delta Kappan*, June 1997, pp. 769–71.

18. Ibid., p. 770.

19. A set of articles appeared in the June 1997 issue of the *Phi Delta Kappan* detailing the background and purpose of these forums, sharing some organizational details and lessons learned, and describing some individual forums. Materials describing how to organize a forum locally are no longer available from Phi Delta Kappa. However, as we write this, they are being revised and updated and (with PDK's permission) will soon be available again. For information on the status of these revised materials, send an e-mail to Phil Harris at pharris@ait.net.

20. Elliot W. Eisner, "The Kind of Schools We Need," *Phi Delta Kappan*, April 2002, p. 580.

21. Anne T. Henderson, "Testimony on NCLB Reauthorization: Effective Strategies for Engaging Parents and Communities in Schools," U.S. Senate Committee on Health, Education, Labor, and Pensions, Wednesday, March 28, 2007. Henderson, a Senior Fellow in the Community Involvement Program, Annenberg Institute for School Reform, is a longtime advocate of parent involvement in the schools, and she offers a range of ideas, some of which are bound to be helpful in your particular situation. A copy of her testimony can be found at http://74.125.95.132/search?q=cache:AGLcoYzo6_MJ:www.ncpie.org/docs/Henderson.Testimony.Senate.March2007.pdf+anne+henderson&cd=4&hl=en&ct=clnk&gl=us. If that's too much to type, try googling the title.

Say What?: An Abbreviated Glossary

> Everyone believes in the [normal] law of errors: the mathematicians, because they think it is an experimental fact; and the experimenters, because they suppose it is a theorem of mathematics.
>
> —Gabriel Lippmann, nineteenth-century physicist

Like Humpty Dumpty, those in the test business sometimes seem to use words to mean whatever they want them to mean. But that's not really a fair criticism. There are clear definitions for specific uses and good reasons for keeping these specialized uses separate. Here are a few definitions of some terms that are common in the literature of testing. Some are no doubt familiar to you already; others might be new. But even the familiar ones are often misused and even more frequently misunderstood. Don't worry, there won't be a quiz, so you don't need to memorize anything. So you can push the demons of "test anxiety" (defined below) back down into the sub-basement of your brain where they belong.

Standardized test. First things first. We've been using the term *standardized test* from the beginning. It's so common in our culture that all of us just read it or hear it and move on. We rarely give it a second thought. The mental image most likely conjured by the term will be something like the SAT—a test booklet, a score sheet with lots of multiple-choice bubbles to fill in, and a follow-up report that gives you both a scaled score and a percentile score (both defined below).

Well, that certainly qualifies as a standardized test, but the term is far more inclusive than that. All the term means is that as many things as possible about a test are kept "standard"—that is, the same for everyone. Same questions, same time limit, same instructions, same scoring, and so on. So your school's tests that meet No Child Left Behind requirements are standardized, as is your state's high school diploma test (if it has one), as is the driver's test your teenage daughter is itching to take. Some of the driving examiners might be "easy" or "tough," but their instructions and training are the same, and the conditions are as standardized as they can be.

Norm-referencing. In nontechnical terms, this means that each student's score is related to the scores of the other test takers. The percentile score mentioned above is a sure sign that you are in the presence of a norm-referenced test. And on such a test, 50 percent of the students will score above the mean and 50 percent below. It's not a failure of the schools, the teachers, or the students. It's a feature of the test design.

Criterion-referencing. A student's scores on a criterion-referenced test specify just how well a student does when measured against a specific benchmark or set of behaviors. Sounds simple, but in practice it has proved to be anything but. One big reason is that specifying a criterion of success for schools is devilishly difficult, and doing so in a way that is measurable by cheap and easy means is probably impossible.

Norming. This odd word that will set off your computer's spell-checker crops up a lot in psychometrics because it refers to the process of creating a norm-referenced test. Simply put, norming or establishing a norm means to set the 50 percent point around which a bell curve arranges itself. Gerald Bracey writes, "To determine the norm, test publishers first try out their questions on students and choose the questions that behave properly. By and large, this means choosing questions that 50 percent of the students miss."[1] If too many students get an item right (or wrong, for that matter), the question doesn't differentiate among the students, and the test makers don't learn much.

Scaled scores. A scaled score is a conversion of a student's raw score (the actual number of items answered correctly) on a test or a version of the test to a common scale. This allows for a numerical comparison to be made among students. Major testing programs use scaled scores to enable them to compare scores from different administrations of a test and from different versions of a test. The SAT scores we have all come to recognize are examples of scaled scores. (Indeed, like IQ scores, SAT scores are standard scores, but we won't be using that term, and it's somewhat technical, so we aren't including it here.) The scores on each SAT subtest are spread out along a scale that ranges from 200 to 800, but no one answered eight hundred questions.

1. Gerald W. Bracey, *Put to the Test: An Educator's and Consumer's Guide to Standardized Testing* (Bloomington, IN: Phi Delta Kappa International, 1998), p. 20.

Percentile scores. Percentiles are comparative scores and have nothing to do with what percent of the items on a test you got correct. Simply put, a percentile score represents the percentage of test takers who score below a certain point. So if your percentile score is 65, then 65 percent of those who took the test scored lower than you did.

Cut scores. These are essentially the "pass/fail" line for a given test. Score above a certain level, you pass; score below, you fail. Unfortunately, cut scores have some inherent problems. The biggest one is that they are absolute, while test scores are always fuzzy (see explanations of measurement error and sampling error, below).

Measurement error. First, just because we have measurement error doesn't mean somebody made a mistake. It's simply the inconsistency that's inherent in measurement. A student who takes a test a second time is very *unlikely* to get the same score—even if the same form of the test is used and even if we could completely erase the student's memory (some teachers think that happens naturally every summer). Measurement error is caused by a whole array of factors: different versions of a single test, a student having a bad day, or a room that's too hot or too cold. But for our purposes, think of it as the random and unpredictable imprecision of any test.[2] If you test a lot of students a lot of times, you can come up with an approximate range for measurement error, and you can say, for example, that a student's score is 75 percent ± 4 percent. If that seems to solve the problem, reread the comments on *cut scores*.

Sampling error. This kind of error has to do with the people, or schools, or districts that we decide to test. It's what the "margin of error" means in most newspaper articles about political polls—an ever present, if often annoying, feature of our nearly three-year presidential campaigns. The magnitude of sampling error depends on the size of the sample you examine, but it has become a big problem for schools only since we started attaching high stakes and serious consequences to test scores for states, districts, schools, and individual students. As the groups we test get smaller, the sampling error grows ever larger.[3] Thus No Child Left Behind's well-meaning requirement (maintained in the Obama administration "blueprint") that specific subgroups of students— e.g., low-income students, minorities, those still learning English—be reported separately has reduced the size of groups that must be reported to as few as thirty or forty students in a category, but not lower. Going any lower would

2. For a solid explanation with a great deal more detail, see Daniel Koretz, *Measuring Up: What Educational Testing Really Tells Us* (Cambridge, MA: Harvard University Press, 2008), pp. 145–64.
3. Ibid., p. 166.

make the sampling error so large that we would have no confidence at all in the inferences we draw from the test scores.

Psychometrics. As we mentioned in a footnote earlier, psychometrics just means "mental measurement," and its practitioners are psychometricians. They are the people who design the tests, but they are also the ones who study their impact and figure out what inferences can be supported by which kinds of tests.

Reliability. Reliability in the world of testing simply means consistency from one administration of a test to the next. But this is one of those words that can lead to problems because, outside the world of testing, we often use "reliable" to mean any number of good and trustworthy things. But in the world of testing, a very bad test can be highly reliable—reliably bad.

Validity. Validity refers to whether a test measures what we think it measures. Actually, the psychometricians refer to this as "content validity," and there are several other kinds of validity that we won't go into here. But it's also important to remember that *tests* are neither valid nor invalid; it's the inferences we make on the basis of test scores that can be said to be valid.[4]

Inference. An inference is simply a conclusion or interpretation that logically follows from a premise. We include the word here, immediately after validity, because in psychometrics it is the inferences we draw from test scores that are said to be valid, not the tests or the scores themselves. Though it seems like a very fine distinction, it's not, and that's how we'll use the term in this book. The best explanation we've found is in *Measuring Up*, by Daniel Koretz.[5]

Bias. Bias is a systematic distortion in test scores that leads to incorrect inferences about what they mean.[6] (Good thing we included the definition of inference where we did!) The key word is *incorrect*. It represents the degree to which the "expected value of a test score deviates from the true value of the object the test seeks to measure."[7] That is, how far off is the test score from what you were trying to measure?

Most of us tend to think of bias in its common usage to refer to unfair judgments about groups of people. And in the past, the scores on many tests

---

4. For a detailed discussion of various kinds of validity, see Sharon L. Nichols and David C. Berliner, *Collateral Damage: How High-Stakes Testing Corrupts America's Schools* (Cambridge, MA: Harvard Education Press, 2007), chap. 5; and Koretz, chap. 9.

5. See Koretz, pp. 216–19.

6. See Koretz, chap. 11.

7. Eric Grodsky, John Robert Warren, and Erika Felts, "Testing and Social Stratification in American Education," *Annual Review of Sociology*, vol. 34, 2008, p. 392.

lent weight to such unfair distinctions. Things have improved a good deal in such areas as question design. But the word has a broader meaning and can refer to scores that are "biased" by such things as excessive or even illicit test preparation. It is important to remember, though, that merely finding a difference between the test scores of two groups doesn't say anything about bias. The inference you draw from that difference may still be a valid one.

Bell curve. Much of the confusion surrounding the "bell curve" has to do with its other name: the normal curve. (It was once called the "normal law of errors," but that's a history lesson for another day.) If it's normal, it's easy to suppose that that must somehow be good or at least the way it's supposed to be. But a normal distribution will arise whenever a set of data is distributed randomly around a mean—equally above and below, with higher values closer to the mean—and the distribution represents the contributions of a large number of small effects.[8] That's all.

Though it is very commonly employed in mental measurement, it is strictly speaking a mathematical entity. Nineteenth-century physicist Gabriel Lippmann is said to have remarked: "Everyone believes in the [normal] law of errors: the mathematicians, because they think it is an experimental fact; and the experimenters, because they suppose it is a theorem of mathematics."

Score spread. Closely related in practice to the creation of the bell curve distribution for test scores, the idea of spreading out test scores so that decisions can be made about those tested has not changed since the earliest days of standardized testing at the dawn of the twentieth century. That's when Alfred Binet's IQ test was adapted and applied (thoughtlessly, in hindsight) to the effort to select the best recruits for the officer corps in World War I.[9]

8. Stephen Jay Gould, *The Mismeasure of Man* (1981; rev. and ex., New York: Norton, 1996), p. 33.
9. W. James Popham, *The Truth about Testing: An Educator's Call to Action* (Alexandria, VA: Association for Supervision and Curriculum Development, 2001), pp. 40–42.

Index

About the Authors

Phillip Harris is currently the executive director of the Association for Educational Communications & Technology. Prior to assuming the leadership of AECT, he was director of the Center for Professional Development at Phi Delta Kappa International. He was on the faculty of Indiana University for twenty-two years serving in both the Psychology Department and the School of Education before becoming a part of Phi Delta Kappa. He received all three of his degrees from Indiana University, completing his Ed.D. in 1967.

Bruce M. Smith attended the Massachusetts Institute of Technology (B.S., 1971); the University of New Hampshire (M.A., 1973); and Indiana University (Ph.D., 1981). He taught writing at Indiana, where he also served as assistant editor of *College English*, the official higher education journal of the National Council of Teachers of English (1977–1981). From 1981 through 2008, he was a member of the editorial staff of the *Phi Delta Kappan*, rising from assistant editor to editor in chief. He maintains an interest in the intersection of educational issues and public policy.

Joan Harris retired in 2010 as a third-grade teacher at University Elementary School in Bloomington, Indiana. She taught first, second, and third grades for over twenty-five years and always found it to be an exciting experience. She has B.S. and M.S. degrees in elementary education from Indiana University and has attended numerous workshops and professional development activities including a special workshop in Problem-Based Learning. In 1997 Joan was recognized by the National Association for the Education of Young Children as the outstanding teacher of the year.